**Books are to be returned on or before
the last date below.**

LONGMAN MEDIEVAL AND RENAISSANCE LIBRARY

General Editors:
CHARLOTTE BREWER, Hertford College, Oxford
N. H. KEEBLE, University of Stirling

Published Titles:

Piers Plowman: An Introduction to the B-Text
James Simpson

Shakespeare's Mouldy Tales: Recurrent Plot Motifs in Shakespearian Drama
Leah Scragg

The Fabliau in English
John Hines

English Medieval Mystics: Games of Faith
Marion Glasscoe

Regaining Paradise Lost
Thomas N. Corns

The Classical Legacy in Renaissance Poetry
Robin Sowerby

Speaking Pictures: English Emblem Books and Renaissance Culture
Michael Bath

Thomas N. Corns

REGAINING
PARADISE LOST

LONGMAN
LONDON AND NEW YORK

Longman Group Limited,
Longman House, Burnt Mill,
Harlow, Essex CM20 2JE, England
and Associated Companies throughout the world.

Published in the United States of America
by Longman Publishing, New York

©Longman Group Limited 1994

First published 1994

ISBN 0 582 066212 CSD
ISBN 0 582 066204 PPR

British Library Cataloguing-in-Publication Data

A catalogue record for this book is
available from the British Library

Library of Congress Cataloging-in-Publication Data

Corns, Thomas N.
    Regaining paradise lost / Thomas Corns.
        p. cm. — (Longman medieval and Renaissance library)
    Includes bibliographical references and index.
    ISBN 0-582-06621-2 (csd). — ISBN 0-582-06620-4 (ppr)
    1. Milton, John, 1608-1674. Paradise lost. I. Title.
II. Series.
    PR3562.C66   1994
    813'.54—dc20   94-2146
                                                                 CIP
                                                                 AC

Set by 5PP in 10/12pt Bembo
Produced by Longman Singapore Publishers (Pte) Ltd.
Printed in Singapore

Contents

g

Preface

Paradise Lost, first published in 1667, strikes those who begin to read it now as a difficult text. Quite probably it always seemed so, and rightly for it makes considerable demands of its readers. Milton appeared to admit its difficulty when he prayed that his 'song' would find 'fit audience . . . though few' (7.31). He was probably thinking primarily of moral fitness, of a godly readership capable of responding to the theological perspective his poem contains. He would have taken for granted that only a small proportion of his compatriots would read it. Indeed, only a minority could read anything. In the mid-seventeenth century, only 40 per cent of men and 20 per cent of women signed their names to documents, rather than endorsing them with their mark.[1] There is a considerable difference in the level of literacy required to make a signature and to read Milton's epic. But the literary culture of Milton's day was quite narrowly circumscribed (though it was certainly widening), and his poetry is the poetry of an educated elite.

Yet even that contemporary elite may well have found *Paradise Lost* challenging. Its publishing history within Milton's lifetime showed some concessions to the reading public. Its fourth issue, in 1668, contained for the first time an explanation of his choice of unrhymed verse, together with the 'arguments' or abstracts of each book. Its printing history in the later seventeenth and the eighteenth centuries indicates both that it commanded a considerable and expanding readership and that its readers required help with understanding the text. From Patrick Hume's annotated edition of 1695 onwards, the poem has accreted a massive commentary tradition. Addison's influential series of essays in *The Spectator* in 1712 presented it in a form accessible to a far wider audience than Milton can have intended or expected.

Of course, by then *Paradise Lost* was being reinterpreted and appropriated by a literary culture at some remove from Milton's own, and the force of much critical effort has been to accommodate readers to its local difficulties, rather than to recontextualise the poem imaginatively in the cultural fabric in which it had its origins. Certainly Milton's English (like Donne's or Shakespeare's) is early modern English and its obscurities need glossing; moreover, Milton's (like Pope's or Eliot's) is a poetry of allusion, and very properly those allusions should be explained, especially for readers less familiar than those of Milton's own age with classical literature and with the Bible. But these are minor difficulties (inconveniences, almost) to be surmounted with a little effort; more challenging are the poem's larger arguments and its intersection with the ideological crises of English radicalism in the 1660s, problems which Addison either did not notice or sought to ignore.

The purpose of this introductory study is restoration; the text is to appear, I hope, with some of the freshness it once had. *Paradise Lost* is now so often regarded as a point of backwards reference, the essential English epic quarried for interesting phrases or idioms or gestures by Keats or by Wordsworth or played off and wittily adapted by Pope. In 1667, though, it was a point of reference forward, scintillating with the challenge of the new, as Milton claimed, pursuing '[t]hings unattempted yet in prose or rhyme' (1.16). It was an *avant guardist* work, as disconcerting in its own age as *The Wasteland* or *Lyrical Ballads* were in theirs. In part that power rests in its new poetic idiom; it is the most confident and ambitious assertion of English neoclassicism in literary art, and it proclaims the supremacy of vernacular Christian poetry over its pagan and classical models. In theological terms, while engaging the controversies central to mid–century Protestantism, it operates too at the very edge of religious speculation. Politically, it articulates, sometimes in necessarily covert form, the revolutionary ideology of the overthrown English republic.

Paradoxically, once we return *Paradise Lost* to its original cultural context it emerges far more strongly as a poem which speaks to our own age, much more so than that pale ghost of Anglican respectability which Addison and his followers conjured from its corpse. Milton's courage commands attention, for this is a work of consummate grace achieved under the devastating fire of Restoration royalism. The text demonstrates how ideologies may, in high art, survive their political eclipse.

I have attempted to reduce annotation and documentation of my argument to a minimum. But this reading owes much to the Milton criticism and scholarship of the last 25 years, and I should like to express my gratitude for earlier work, pre-eminently that of Alastair Fowler, whose edition of 1968 pervades much of what I have to say; and to the studies of Dennis Burden, John Carey, Dennis Danielson, William Empson, Stanley Fish, Christopher Hill, G. K. Hunter, John Leonard, Michael Lieb, David Loewenstein, Regina Schwartz, Stella Revard and James Turner, whose insights and scholarship form essential ingredients in my view of *Paradise Lost*. In a different kind of book, they would have been heavily cited; here I can offer only general acknowledgment and commend them to those who would read further. I should like particularly to thank Neil Keeble, joint editor of this series, and Gordon Campbell, who both read all the manuscript, and Peter Kitson, who read most of it, commenting (always encouragingly) on its errors and omissions.

NOTES

1.   David Cressy, *Literacy and the Social Order: Reading and Writing in Tudor and Stuart England* (Cambridge: Cambridge University Press, 1980), p. 72.

Acknowledgements

The author and publishers would like to thank the editors of the *Revue Belge de Philologie et d'Histoire* for their kind permission to reprint in Chapter 5 some material published in that periodical.

For Robert and Richard

Chapter 1

God

> here nature first begins
> Her farthest verge, and Chaos to retire
> As from her outmost works a broken foe
> With tumult less and with less hostile din,
> That Satan with less toil, and now with ease
> Wafts on the calmer wave by dubious light
> And like a weather-beaten vessel holds
> Gladly the port, though shrouds and tackle torn;
> Or in the emptier waste, resembling air,
> Weighs his spread wings, at leisure to behold
> Far off the empyreal heaven, extended wide
> In circuit, undetermined square or round,
> With opal towers and battlements adorned
> Of living sapphire, once his native seat;
> And fast by hanging in a golden chain
> This pendant world, in bigness as a star
> Of smallest magnitude close by the moon.
> Thither full fraught with mischievous revenge,
> Accursed, and in a cursed hour he hies.

$$(2.1037–55)^1$$

This is the reader's first clear view of heaven – Satan, of course, has seen it before, the last time as he tumbled from it with the other rebel angels. The reader has had some hint of its characteristics a little earlier: the narrator has told us that the 'trodden gold' of its pavement was much admired by Mammon even before his fall (1.679–84). Satan views the earth for the first time; the reader, who of course regards it daily from a terrestrial perspective, is invited to view it afresh, as if from a remote position in space. After the horrors Satan and, vicariously, the reader have endured over the earlier 1800 lines, its beauty appears at once arresting, soothing, and poignant. The geography of heaven is and will remain mysterious: neither Satan nor the narrator may discern whether its outline constitutes a circle or a square. But Satan will come to know earth as intimately as ourselves.

After the bizarre 'darkness visible' of hell, the randomness of Chaos, and the nightmarish uncertainties of those obtrusive and active allegories, Sin and Death, the modality of which defies a confident classification, the realms of light refresh both Satan and the reader. Doubt, chance, indeterminacy, obscurity both literal and metaphorical are displaced by the hard edge of a clear light by which heaven and earth may be discerned and which in turn is reflected by the refulgencies of opal, sapphire and gold.

'*This* pendant world' retains a full deictic force. Satan comes hither to us. For the reader, the external view, though vital in that it establishes the proximity and connection of earth to heaven, is imaginative and provisional. It also allows us to see the external threats surrounding our world. A little earlier, as Satan traverses with difficulty the dark abyss, the narrator in an aside anticipates the 'bridge of wondrous length' by which Sin and Death will link hell (again, note the deictic force) to 'this frail world'. Satan, disarmingly, approaches earth as a merchantman, with tattered sails, returns home after an epic of commercial adventure. What is carried in his hold, however, are not the riches of the orient; rather he is 'full fraught', that is heavily laden, with 'mischievous revenge'.

The space journey and the distant perspective it affords are quite familiar elements of the western literary tradition; Milton is not alone in effecting such an imaginative *tour de force*. But closer to Milton both in time and in high seriousness than, for example, Chaucer's *House of Fame*[2] is Abraham Cowley's extraordinary 'pindaric ode', 'The Extasie', first published in 1656. Comparison discloses important differences of emphasis. In 'The Extasie' the speaker, disembodied by the temporary separation of soul from body, takes the route the prophet Elijah took when he was carried to heaven in a chariot of fire (2 Kings 2:11). Just as Milton's attention in *Paradise Lost* frequently fixes on the end of the world, Cowley regards Elijah's fiery transport as an anticipation of the raising of '*Phoenix Nature* aged grown' to heaven after apocalyptic incineration.[3] Significantly, though, Cowley takes a very different kind of comfort from an extraterrestrial perspective which, as in *Paradise Lost*, discloses the smallness of this world in the enormity of space:

> How small the biggest Parts of *Earths* Proud *Tittle* show!
> Where shall I find the noble *Brittish* Land?
> Lo, I at last a *Northern Spec* espie,
>> Which in the *Sea* does lie,
>> And seems a *Grain* o'th' *Sand*
> For this will any *sin*, or *Bleed*?
> Of *Civil Wars* is this the *Meed*?
>> And is it this, alas, which we
> (Oh *Irony* of *Words*!) do call *Great Britanie*?.

(stanzas 2–3)

Cowley's concern is to take and offer comfort from the triviality of the earth and especially Britain from a vantage point approaching that of God. In the larger view, which is a view both of time and space, the mutable world ends incorporated once more into the Godhead, its temporary sins and agonies reduced to a minor significance.

Milton's view is perhaps richer, but like Cowley's it depends on positing earth's relationship to heaven. His ideological predicament in the 1660s quite closely parallels Cowley's in the 1650s. Each has come to recognise the bankruptcy of the political causes in the advancement of which they had expended their creative energies, endured (albeit short-lived) incarceration, and had risked far graver penalties. For nothing. Each witnessed the triumph of the enemy. Cowley effects his ideological escape through contemplating the transience of that which had seemed so important as Britain becomes a '*Grain* o'th' *Sand*' not worth contention. Milton provisionally resolves his by locating the tiny brilliance of the world, soon to be lost to Satan, the archetype of all ungodly adversaries, next to the enormous magnificence of a heaven which can be witnessed only by space-travellers or by the imaginative revelation of the seer-poet. The issue of scale is central to the tactic. Milton is never unworldly; he never denigrates the beauty of the created world and the value of human experiences, emotions and courage. The loss of prelapsarian perfection and the impoverishment of human experience by pain, sin and defeat are depicted as poignantly tragic, incapable of an easy transcendence, for they touch the godly more sharply than the unregenerate. The horrors surrounding and eventually overwhelming this pendant world are, however, mitigated by the unthreatened and immutable presence of heaven. Earth is to heaven as the smallest star, seen by the human eye, is to the moon. Whatever Satan's achievements in this little world, that larger entity remains unchallengeable (but remote) as a final resort for those who persevere and a final reservoir of redemption for a fallen creation.

Milton's theology, the theology of the defeated, attributes all power to an invisible and invincible agency which outranks worldly and Satanic evil. Judgement, reward and punishment remain after the Fall the most important roles of the deity. Milton writes after the Atonement; the incarnate Son has discharged the larger debt incurred at the fall of Adam and Eve; the godly must now merely endure and await the inevitable reward. Uncompromising about the grimness of human experience, Milton represents the horrors to be endured by Christ's saints in the period between his death and his second coming as sometimes worse than his own grisly end. When Adam puts this proposition to Michael, his response concedes the point but invokes heaven's action:

> [Adam speaks] Will they not deal
> Worse with his followers than with him they dealt?
> Be sure they will, said the angel . . .
>
> (12.483–5)

Some devotional writers, especially of the Catholic tradition, stressed that Christ's suffering surpassed that of others in that his finer characteristics made him more sensible to agony. Milton will have none of that. The dogma of the Incarnation requires the Son to suffer as people suffer, and palpably some suffer worse torment than Christ's own agony, not least in the torment of the protracted triumph of one's ungodly enemies. Milton's closest political associates had paid gross penalties at the hands of those ungodly, and he must have known at least slightly all the regicides throttled and disembowelled in 1660, since all had been prominent in the early 1650s when he worked for the Council of State (see Chapter 6). Michael's comments could be a gloss on the conduct of some at the obscene ritual of their own martyrdoms. Most memorably, General Thomas Harrison, who had reminded his judge that the execution of the King was not a thing done in a corner and who had assured his jeerers that he carried still the

Good Old Cause in his bosom and would seal it 'with his blood', died, as Pepys observed, 'looking as cheerfully as any man could in that condition'.[4]

The Restoration government was at pains to stress that General Harrison's evident optimism was premissed on the palpably mistaken assumption that he was shortly to be physically resurrected and that he would return with Christ to complete his revolutionary objectives, with the intention that his followers should be disappointed by his failure to reappear.[5] *Paradise Lost* shows no confidence about the imminence of Christ's second coming. That appears as a certain but remote source of comfort to the godly wayfarer in the fallen world, a solution not to be realised before much horror has been experienced and endured.

This remote postponement contrasts sharply both with Milton's earliest accounts of God's involvement with human history, and with *Paradise Regained* (1671), by which time only Satan and his associates regard the question as pertinent.[6] In his ode 'On the Morning of Christ's Nativity', composed some 38 years before the first publication of *Paradise Lost*, he had linked the Incarnation with the Second Coming. 'Nature' is represented as mistaking the nature of Christ's first mission, believing instead that her role is completed (as it will be on his return), and briefly and provisionally the poet's voice endorses this sentiment: 'lep'rous sin will melt from earthly mould,/And hell itself will pass away'.[7] In his first prose polemic, *Of Reformation* (1641), he envisages, not the passing of hell (with its optimistic assumption that perhaps all souls will be delivered from it), but the sealing of hell, with the Anglican bishops and other enemies of the godly incarcerated within it. Meanwhile, the godly themselves 'shall clasp inseparable Hands with *joy*, and *blisse* in over measure for ever.'[8]

That same expectation of 'joy and eternal bliss' (12.551) remains a potent and reiterated motif of *Paradise Lost*. But it is a postponed restitution, without the urgent sense, felt in *Of Reformation*, that events in England were rushing towards that climax in step with God's own schedule. Michael concludes his long prophetic vision of the suffering of the godly with:

> so shall the world go on,
> To good malignant, to bad men benign,
> Under her own weight groaning till the day
> Appear of respiration to the just,

> And vengeance to the wicked, at return
> Of him so lately promised to thy aid
> The woman's seed, obscurely then foretold,
> Now amplier known thy saviour and thy Lord,
> Last in the clouds from heaven to be revealed.
>
> (12.537–45)

The phrasing indicates perhaps a certain frustration with the enigmatic nature of the Book of Genesis (after all, only hours have passed since Adam received the first, rather veiled, promise of divine intervention in future times). Dramatically, concluding the horrors Michael has revealed, it is more than sufficient to cheer Adam's gloom; '[g]reatly in peace of thought' (12.558) he may now leave Paradise, though he foresees (as the Christian tradition often does) that the victories available to the godly are to be of a paradoxical kind, 'by things deemed weak/Subverting worldly strong' (12.567–8). The triumphs anticipated in *Of Reformation* are displaced by a long vista of saintly martyrs repeating the sufferings of Christ. Though Adam thanks Michael for a 'prediction' which has 'soon . . . /Measured this transient world, the race of time,/Till time stand fixed' (12.553–5), that measuring seems decidedly indeterminate.

The final reckoning, though postponed *sine die*, nevertheless recurs at symbolically privileged points of the poem. It is rehearsed in the opening lines, albeit obliquely:

> Of man's first disobedience, and the fruit
> Of that forbidden tree, whose mortal taste
> Brought death into the world, and all our woe,
> With loss of Eden, till one greater man
> Restore us, and regain the blissful seat,
> Sing heavenly Muse . . .
>
> (1.1–6)

The passage is probably more complicated than at first it may seem. Of course, the second Adam, the greater man, is a Pauline formula for the incarnate Christ.[9] But the nature of the restoration is problematic. Fowler suggests that it means both replacement in a state of grace and a making of amends for human sin.[10] It implies, too, a physical and political action, the reinstatement of people into original possessions from which they had been excluded (*OED* 4b), in the 1660s at the very least a warm issue.

The connection of the restoration with a geographical location for me makes this perhaps the primary force of the line (though not to the exclusion of the other significations). Christ's Atonement, then, validates humankind's return to a state of grace, quits their outstanding debts (both of which are effected immediately by the Atonement itself, though Adam and his heirs had access to grace from immediately after the fall, if they chose to cooperate with it; on grace, see below, Chapter 3.) But it also promises a restoration to paradise. What does Milton mean? Is he equating the new earth promised in the Book of Revelations (Rev. 21:1) with the lost paradise of Eden? Or is heaven itself, the eventual destination of the godly, the new paradise to which mankind will be restored? That equation is perhaps premissed on Christ's words from the Cross to the penitent malefactor, an account which also invokes an image of political restoration:

> Luke 23:42 And he said unto Jesus, Lord, remember me when thou comest into thy kingdom.
> 43 And Jesus said unto him, Verily I say unto thee, To day shalt thou be with me in paradise.

In the privileged dialogue of the Father and the Son, in which the Godhead ponders over the prospect of human history, the former explicitly endorses the notion of the second Adam developed in the narrator's comments which open the poem:

> be thou in Adam's room
> The head of all mankind, though Adam's son.
> As in him perish all men, so in thee
> As from a second root shall be restored,
> As many as are restored, without thee none.

> (3.285–9)

The conclusion of this restoration is clear: heaven and earth will be reconstructed, and, presumably in the latter, 'the just shall dwell,' enjoying 'golden days,' as if in compensation for the 'tribulations long' which they experienced while witnessing to the truth in the fallen world. 'Then' (presumably after that thousand year reign) 'thou thy regal sceptre shalt lay by' and 'God shall be all in all' (334–41). Most of this is based upon commonplace Protestant exegesis of the Book of Revelation, though that riddling last phrase, taken from Paul (1 Cor. 15:28), will need further attention (see Chapter 4).

However, as the Father and the Son discuss both the Atonement and the Millennium, they do so within a frame of reference which excludes the human notion of time. As has frequently been remarked, the Son speaks as if his involvement in the saving of the world and the liberation of the godly requires, not two visits (the Incarnation and the Second Coming), but one: 'Then [I] with the multitude of my redeemed/Shall enter heaven long absent, and return' (260–1). The Father retells the Son what the Son has just told the Father, but he does so with a greater precision. However, what we encounter is a series of events, the order of which seems clear, but the temporal relation between which seems uncertain (274–341). In neither account is there a suggestion of the time span between the stages: what in Michael's narrative to Adam seems almost interminable, in the Godhead's account seems unrelated to time.

Empson in his anti-Christian account offers a rather jaundiced reading of this passage, concluding that the Son 'does not know what is going to happen, except for a triumph at which he can rejoice.'[11] However, Father and Son speak in accord, the latter initiating the prophetic mode, the former confirming and extending it, adding to the sense of exhilaration associated with the godly's experience of the end of the world. The absence of detail about Christ's spectacular and tortured death scarcely surprises: Milton had every reason to assume a familiarity with such things among the godly – enough of them had recently endured it – and he may well have assumed that they, very reasonably, would prefer to take such sufferings as read. Neither Michael nor the Godhead holds out any promise that the epoch for such repeated suffering will be short-lived.

Indeed, the sequence of events which closes the epic leaves its readers with an abiding image, not of a paradise imminently to be regained, but of human responsibility in the fallen world extending almost infinitely before them. Michael offers Adam an alternative paradise, but it is to be achieved only through self-discipline and a sort of spiritual self-help:

> This [i.e. 'that to obey is best' (12.561)] having
>   learned, thou hast attained the sum
> Of wisdom . . .
>   only add
> Deeds to thy knowledge answerable, add faith,
> Add virtue, patience, temperance, add love,

By name to come called Charity, the soul
Of all the rest: then wilt thou not be loath
To leave this Paradise, but shalt possess
A paradise within thee, happier far.

(12.575–87)

Note the imperative mood: Adam must, in a sense, construct
his role as a godly wayfarer from the parts Michael lists. Only
'then' may that interior paradise be possessed. Nor will it have
the physical, material splendour from which Adam and Eve are
poignantly excluded. The last occurrence of the word 'paradise',
like our last view of Paradise, is in a context of exclusion. The
reader shares Adam and Eve's backward glance, seeing as they see:

They looking back, all the eastern side beheld
Of Paradise, so late their happy seat,
Waved over by that flaming brand, the gate
With dreadful faces thronged and fiery arms . . .

(12.641–4)

Not only 'dreadful' but also 'thronged' arrests the reader's atten-
tion. 'Dreadful' is a word often applied to aspects of the Godhead
(OED2), though it sounds frighteningly interdictive. The guilty
Adam had previously found the Son's voice 'dreadful' (10.779).
But Satan, too, seems dreadful (1.130), as do the ranks of fallen
angels (1.564), and Death's dart (2.672). Again, Milton does speak
of the 'throng' of good angels (4.831, 5.650) as well as of the fallen
(10.453). Yet elsewhere the verbal force of 'throng' is reserved for
the fallen, suggestive of an unnatural plenitude of beings. The
monstrously diminished fallen angels '[t]hrong numberless, like
that pygmean race,/Beyond the Indian mount, or faerie elves'
(1.780–1) into Pandaemonium, all access to which is described, very
shortly before, as 'thronged' (1.761). The 'flaming brand' and the
'fiery arms' are in part at least required by the source material
– explicitly, the angels sent to guard Paradise are cherubim,
elsewhere associated with fires (6.413), and the symbol of inter-
diction is 'a flaming sword, which turned every way, to keep the
way of the tree of life' (Gen. 3:24). But fire is the present realm of
the fallen angels: the first and abiding recollection of them within
the poem is of them 'rolling in the fiery gulf' (1.52).

The final vision of Paradise has long since provoked the thought
that the angels that now infest it are not good ones but some of

Satan's band (Fowler, 12.633–41n). But that surely is not quite the
point. As Adam and Eve and the readers look on the host, they
do so without any understanding of who they are, what their
mission is, and why such numbers. The opening lines of Book
9 had warned,

> No more of talk where God or angel guest
> With man, as with his friend, familiar used
> To sit indulgent.
>
> (1–3)

Indeed not. God has returned primarily to judge (though second-
arily to comfort); Michael has come, but to offer a vision of
happiness almost infinitely postponed; and these other angels could
just as easily be devils for all that Adam can see or know. 'Familiar
angel,' as Fowler noted, meant guardian angel, and 'familiar' could
also carry the notion 'on a family footing'. These cherubim of
the expulsion are unfamiliar in every sense: what they guard is
not Adam but the tree of life from which he and his heirs are
excluded. Far from entering and conversing intimately in the
family home of Adam and Eve, they expel them from that
home. Their disposition and their obtrusive display of force
are bafflingly unfamiliar. Previously, God had taken measures to
ensure that large-scale military activity did not disrupt Paradise
(4.990–1004); now he has installed a considerable garrison. Can
guarding the tree (from whom?) require such numbers and such
vigilance? The behaviour of angels and the motivation behind
it are no longer to be represented to humankind in humanly
comprehensible terms.

But are Adam and Eve so alone? As Adam draws comfort from
the vision Michael has extended to him, he concludes:

> Henceforth I learn, that to obey is best,
> And love with fear the only God, to walk
> As in his presence, ever to observe
> His providence, and on him sole depend . . .
>
> (12.561–4)

They leave Paradise, conscious both of the obligations of choice
confronting the displaced wayfarer, of their loneliness, but also of
an inner force:

> The world was all before them, where to choose
> Their place of rest, and providence their guide:

They hand in hand with wandering steps and slow,
Through Eden took their solitary way.

(12.646–9)

'Solitary,' presumably, because, though they are a couple, they
are unaccompanied by God or angels. Adam had resolved, not
to walk in God's presence, but *as* (that is, *as if*) in his presence.
They have 'providence', though that term seems to include rather
less than once it may seemed to have done. Certainly, it includes
a recognition of the promise of the Atonement and of the final
reward for the godly and it includes the strength by which they
may resist the onslaughts of temporal power and oppression. But
it does not include the certainty of any special providence extended
to them.

The contrast with how Milton had used the term in the 1640s
and 1650s is quite marked. Certainly, Milton was more cautious
than some in identifying the direct hand of a providential Godhead
in shaping English history in the mid-century. For example,
he reproves Charles I for interpreting a political or military
development as evidence of God's providence towards him:

> No evil can befall the Parlament or Citty, but he positively interprets
> it a judgement upon them for his sake; as if the very manuscript
> of Gods judgements had bin deliverd to his custody and exposition.
> . . . And . . . he takes upon him perpetually to unfold the secret and
> unsearchable Mysteries of high Providence.
>
> (*Eikonoklastes*, CPW 3. 563–4)

Yet Milton in the same tract can play the King's game, counter-
asserting that 'Good Providence . . . curbs the raging of proud
Monarchs' (379). In the twilight of the republic, he asserts that the
English people have been 'deliverd by [God] from a king, and not
without wondrous acts of his providence, insensible and unworthie
of those high worthies' (*Readie and Easie Way*, second edition, CPW
7, revised edition, 450). The sentiment is less keenly felt than by
some shallower thinkers, and less keenly than by those who had
confronted the enemy in arms and felt the extraordinariness of
their deliverance.[12] Yet the reader of Milton's prose surely has a
sense that he shares the view of victorious contemporaries, that
God's special mercy is available to the godly. Adam takes with
him no such certainties into the fallen world. Michael's vision
contains some elements of temporal punishment to the ungodly

(as in the treatment of the civilisation wiped out by the Flood), and sometimes the godly are saved and even those of no conspicuous merit may obtain the fruits of his 'mercy' (12.346). Yet the lasting impression he must take is of a mercy postponed: the *imitatio Christi* which the wayfarer, fortified by inner strength, may be obliged to make is one of resolute suffering: providence offers no promise of temporal victory.

The larger configuration of the universe Milton describes exhibits curious contradictions. All human aspiration hangs on the presence and the promise afforded by the Godhead and by the heaven he invests and where mankind is eventually to dwell with him. Before the Fall, it seemed quite close, the golden chain that links them apparent to incoming Satan and imaginable by Milton and his readers. The prospect before Adam and Eve is bounded by the now rather desolate horizons of the fallen world. The Godhead is hidden and restoration almost infinitely postponed.

The issue of time is a vital one. As Guibbory has well illustrated, seventeenth-century perspectives were quite varied, but much was premissed on a sense of time's finiteness:

> When Archbishop James Ussher began his *Annals of the World* (1658) with the confident announcement that history began with Creation on Sunday 'the twenty third day of *Octob.* in the year of the Julian Calendar, 710,' 4,004 years before Christ, he assumed, like many writers in the seventeenth century, that temporal experience had shape and order, that history revealed a pattern that human being could comprehend. With its providentially fixed beginning at Creation and its end at the Last Judgement, history had a definite, limited shape. The order was there; it had only to be discovered and charted. [13]

But Ussher is a scholar: his confidence is earned, arrived at by the persistent and dedicated application of one of the finest intellects of his age to a problem which he and his contemporaries perceived as tractable to such resolution. Three of his publications consider at some length the question of the age of the world and of the relationship between Bible chronology and the chronology of events, primarily in Mediterranean history, documented elsewhere. The process is essentially Baconian, thoroughly in the spirit of intellectual enquiry of the new science of his age. The Bible is a text, to be interpreted (among other strategies) as a source of dates and events and biographies. In his *Annales veteris testamenti* (London, 1650), in the posthumously published *Annals of the World*

(London, 1658) and *Chronologia Sacra* (Oxford, 1660), Ussher works backwards from the life-spans of the earliest patriarchs to establish the beginnings of time, and relates later Biblically described events to contemporary events documented particularly in Greek and Roman history.

Milton's Puritan associates certainly retained some respect for Ussher. He was among the small group of episcopalians nominated to the Westminster Assembly of Divines, convoked by Long Parliament to reform English Protestantism (he was at that time Archbishop of Armagh). In a period of particularly acute anti-episcopal activity, he met with Cromwell in an attempt to moderate the attack, and was courteously received and listened to.[14] Moreover, when Milton himself had cause to answer Ussher, he did so with a caution and an evasiveness which contrasts sharply with his characteristic treatment of prelatical adversaries.[15]

4004 BC as a putative date for the beginning of the world: the notion is not some absurd whimsy indicative of the primitivism of our intellectual forefathers. It was a suggestion from a fine and very widely respected scholar who sought to tie what we may regard as remote and mythic events into the timeframe by which humanistic historians perceived the history of Mediterranean culture. Moreover, the venture was shared by others. Either this larger concern or, possibly, Ussher's own work may well have shaped the view of history Michael vouchsafes to Adam.

The primary impact of the Bible chronologers is to make time seem finite and imaginable in human terms. Adam is not so remote. I am forty-three years old; my first-born grandparent was born over a century ago; on Ussher's reckoning, Adam lived a mere sixty centuries ago. If the millennium is similarly calculable, in centuries rather than aeons – more urgently still, if it is perceived as imminent – then the timespan of the human experience (perhaps, of the human experiment) shrinks to one which is almost reassuringly tractable to human understanding. But take off the *terminus ad quem*, the end of time, and before us lie deserts, not quite of eternity, but of an unconscionable range of time. The effect is profoundly disconcerting, especially for those who anticipate that that vastness will be occupied by the rarely mitigated suffering of the godly. When the world seemed short-lived, such pessimism could be endured; discount its conclusion, and the misery deepens. Its only real mitigation is that, for the individual, the experience lasts merely a lifetime. The millenarianism of Milton's earliest political pamphlet, *Of Reformation* (London, 1641), had offered an image of Christ's return in judgement:

> when thou the Eternall and shortly-expected King shalt open the Clouds to judge the severall Kingdomes of the World, and . . . shalt put an end to all Earthly *Tyrannies,* proclaiming thy universal and milde *Monarchy* through Heaven and Earth.
>
> (*CPW* 1. 616)

Instead, in *Paradise Lost*, the godly make their way through an evil-dominated world which is to be their abode *sine die*. Milton's vision is a rich and complex one; ultimately, it is premissed on that act of faith and imagination cited at the beginning of this chapter. Yet that sense of proximity to a validating and transcendent heaven is persistently challenged and sometimes overwhelmed by a sense of remoteness and a recognition that Christ's kingdom is hidden or postponed. Wonder is elbowed aside by the need for Christian fortitude and perseverance in the concluding images of the poem.

THE FATHER AND THE SON

So far I have spoken, with a purposeful evasiveness, of 'God' or 'the Godhead'. Milton's theology, however, differentiates between the constituents of that Godhead at some length and in ways which have stimulated considerable unresolved controversy. Much of that debate focusses on the relationship between *Paradise Lost* and *De Doctrina Christiana*. The latter, a Latin treatise of over a quarter of a million words, constitutes a sustained exercise in Biblical exegesis intended to define true doctrine through the reconciliation of Biblical texts to one another. Unpublished in Milton's lifetime, it was rediscovered in 1823 during the reorganisation of some late-seventeenth-century state papers, and on its publication in 1825 its heterodoxy (indeed heresy) on a number of key areas of Christian belief was immediately and widely recognised. Milton's status as the leading celebrant of English Protestantism required certain urgent qualifications.[16]

The critical controversy concerning the relationship between the epic and the treatise admits of three major positions. One is well indicated by the title of its most signal exposition, Maurice Kelley's *This Great Argument: A Study of Milton's 'De Doctrina*

Christiana' as a Gloss upon 'Paradise Lost' (Princeton: Princeton UP, 1941). Another, represented by the position of Patrides, Hunter, Adamson and Campbell, argues that the treatise relates very imperfectly to the epic.[17] Campbell further maintains that the treatise is itself an incomplete text which would have received further revision to render it more coherent. The third position, that assumed by Hunter since 1991, cuts the Gordian knot rather differently: the case for Milton's authorship, in his current view, is unproven; questions of provenance are uncertain; and, since points of disagreement between the treatise and other texts which are assuredly part of the Miltonic canon exist, the treatise may be set aside, and possibly may be attributed to one of Milton's contemporaries.[18]

In our present uncertainty, I intend to proceed primarily by invoking the source of what the original readers of *Paradise Lost* may have known about Milton's notions of the Godhead, namely the evidence of that text.

Milton's fullest representation of the Godhead comes in Book 3, in which we see the Father (whom Milton sometimes simply calls 'God') and the Son in dialogue. This, in terms of the theology of the poem, is its most important section, and I suspect that only the doctrinal significance of what Milton has them say would have prompted him to represent them (and especially the Father) in such a human activity as conversation with each other. For the most part within the poem Milton's representation of the Father reflects a sense of awed bewilderment at the boundlessness of his power and extent, and at the mystery with which he surrounds himself. Moreover, contemporaneously, Protestants, particularly those of a puritan tendency, were deeply agitated by any attempt to represent the Godhead in material forms. Of course, they felt an animosity to the religious iconography characteristic of contemporary Catholic practices in devotional fields of the visual arts and a contempt for those icons remaining in English churches from their Catholic days. But we know that they entertained a special concern about the demeaning and, in terms of seventeenth-century Protestant theology, simple-minded representation of the Father. For example, in 1630, in one of the best known acts of iconoclasm from the period of the personal rule of Charles I, Henry Sherfield, recorder of the borough of Salisbury, broke a window in his parish church with his walking stick on the grounds that it represented God 'in the form of an old man'. His subsequent trial before the Star Chamber became the occasion for the Laudian assertion of where authority should lie within the Church, though, interestingly, when the window was mended, Charles I instructed that plain glass be used, even though the stained glass could have been repaired.[19] Sherfield's own religious predilections are unknown, but what the incident shows is that the distaste for such crude anthropomorphism extended to the prelatical wing of Protestant opinion.

Yet Milton, in seeking to associate the doctrinal exposition of Book 3 with the authoritative voice of the Godhead, runs the risk of making human and specific some aspects of the Trinity which elsewhere he leaves decorously uncertain. While this allows him to read his version of the doctrines of the Atonement and of salvation into the record of right religion, the price is the initiation of nagging (but not insuperable) problems about the Miltonic notion of the Trinity.

Through a long section of Book 3, the Father and the Son give each other information (usually of a predictive kind) and they ask each other questions. In the human context the pragmatics of such an exchange usually involves a disparity of knowledge. Characteristically, in conversation, we try not to tell people what they already know, nor, except rhetorically, do we ask questions when we know the answers. However, as we shall see, Milton has some stratagems to mitigate the side effects of his chosen mode of discourse.

The section consists of five major speeches:

1   80–134; the Father foretells the fall of Adam and Eve; he defines the relationship of foreknowledge and predestination; he differentiates the sentence on humankind from that on the fallen angels.
2   144–66; the Son poses the question of how mankind may be saved without abolishing creation and without allowing Satan a local victory.
3   168–216; the Father, briefly setting aside those who are spe-cially elect, explains how grace will operate synergistically with those of fallen humankind who pray and repent; he introduces the doctrine of the Atonement.
4   227–65; the Son volunteers to assume the role and the suffering

of fallen humankind; he foretells his own victory over death and his triumphant return to heaven, when all divine anger towards humankind will be utterly eliminated.

5   274–343; the Father foretells the course of the Incarnation in more detail; he describes the Last Judgement and the millennium and the final phase of human history in which 'God shall be all in all'.

Milton tells us that this exposition is not for the benefit of the Godhead but for the edification and understanding of the inhabitants of heaven (and indirectly, through the medium of his divinely inspired verse, of the fallen humans who constitute Milton's readers). All heaven is listening, and he explicitly remarks, between speeches 4 and 5:

> Admiration seized
> All heaven, what this might mean, and whither tend
> Wondering.
>
> (271-3)

Speech 5, in its greater detail, substantially glosses speech 4 for the benefit, not of the Son, but of the circumambient hearers. It is crucial that the doctrines of the Incarnation and the Atonement are largely established by the Son. This associates the Son with the future of the world; further, it associates the ultimate salvation of humankind not with the Father but with the Son.

What of the questions which the Father and Son ask each other? The first one establishes that their questions have nothing to do with differentials in the divine economy of knowledge: 'Only begotten Son, seest thou what rage/Transports our adversary . . .' (80-1). Since we are told the Son sits next to the Father and since he can see from his high throne Satan's progress through the cosmos and since, anyway, he is omniscient, he does of course *know* that the Son sees Satan's progress as surely as he does himself. It supports the brutal pun on 'transports' (meaning both 'brings' and 'upsets') and it allows the reader to relish the dramatic irony that, though Satan believes he has heroically escaped, both Father and Son know his flight from hell is at their permission. Crucially, though, it establishes that questions between Father and Son do not imply ignorance. This point is neatly and precisely confirmed much later in the poem when the Son returns to heaven after passing judgement on Adam and Eve:

> To him [i.e, to the Father] with swift ascent he up returned,
> Into his blissful bosom reassumed
> In glory as of old, to him appeased
> All, though all-knowing, what passed with man
> Recounted, mixing intercession sweet.

(10.224-8)

Thus Milton explicitly describes the Father and the Son talking to each other about a matter about which both already know all that there is to know; the exchange remains purposeful in that the mercy and the kindness which are primarily associated with the Son are represented as pervading the Son's account.

The rest of speech 1 consists of a series of questions in which the Father justifies his actions against both angels and humankind by indicating that no alternative would be consonant with the first principles on which God's justice is founded. The Son replies with further questions which define the problems which that justice has to negotiate, how punishment may be reconciled with salvation. Note the Father's response to these questions: 'All hast thou spoken as my thoughts are, all/As my eternal purpose hath decreed' (171-2). Yet the Son's thoughts had been questions, not proposals; but they are questions which can only be resolved as the Father has 'decreed' they shall be resolved, through the action of grace in conjunction with the free will of the godly whose actions in prayer and repentance activate its influence on themselves.

The dialogue manifests two emphases within the power and glory of the Godhead. Those aspects associated with the Father tend towards providence and towards justice. Those associated with the Son tend towards self-sacrifice and mercy. I believe Milton would like us to respect this vision as a difficult metaphor at the edge of human understanding. When, before speech 4, the Son is spoken of as renewing his 'dearest mediation' (226) on behalf of humankind, Milton is not postulating a disagreement of purpose or of values between discrete entities; rather, he tries to suggest the complex and potent synthesis of love and justice which constitutes the core of his vision of the divine.

Milton's depiction of the Father manifests at times an uneasy relationship between the metaphoric structures he has inherited from the Bible and the larger, more resonant and more potent notions which characterise Milton's (and other *avant guardist* contemporary theologians') more abstract ponderings on the issues. 'The Father', 'the Son', 'the only begotten' – a human paternalism persistently intrudes into the conceptual framework scripture provides. At its most disconcerting, Father and Son resemble a family alliance effecting a boardroom coup, as when the Son is introduced to a surprised angelic community unaware of his existence as the figure to whom they must 'bow/All knees in heaven' (5.607–8). However, Milton preempts some criticism by having Raphael explain that his narrative is consciously presented in terms comprehensible to humans (5.570–4). Anyway, the Father there seeks to tempt his angelic legions to revolt. Though angelic understanding in some respects differs from human understanding, angels are nevertheless creatures susceptible to the same promptings and the same ethical crises as humans. The rather anthropomorphic (or perhaps angelomorphic) way in which Milton has the Father anoint and enthrone the Son seems perhaps acceptable as an appropriate temptation for the political and hierarchical creatures he represents the angels to be.

Elsewhere in the relationship between Father and Son the Father's role suggests an overwhelming potency which sanctions, animates and initiates the actions of the Son. Thus, on the eve of the third and final day of the war in heaven, he addresses the Son:

> Effulgence of my glory, Son beloved,
> Son in whose face invisible is beheld
> Visibly, what by deity I am,
> And in whose hand what by decree I do,
> Second omnipotence . . .
> Go then thou mightiest of thy Father's might,
> Ascend my chariot . . .
>
> (6.680–4, 710–11)

'In whose face invisible is beheld,/Visibly, what by deity I am': the problems and the paradoxes abound, defining this as a domain beyond the realm of human language and human understanding. 'Invisible', presumably, because at this point both Father and Son sit withdrawn; but that face is beheld by the Father and will be beheld at other times both during the Incarnation and in other dealings the Son is to have with the world. Even 'Effulgence of my glory' is puzzling. 'Effulgence', seemingly a word of Miltonic coinage and one which antedates cognate terms like 'effulgent'

(*OED*), means presumably a brilliant shining forth of the glory of God; but contemporaneously 'glory' could mean effulgence, too (*OED*, s.v. 'Glory', sub., sig. 6). The paradox of 'second omnipotence' indicates that here we are close to the mysteries at the heart of the Trinity. If there is omnipotence, complete power over everything, then, in terms of human logic, there can be no second omnipotence because the first omnipotence would have power over it. The relationship of the Son to the figure who 'owns' the 'chariot of paternal deity' (6.750) is quite carefully set outside the realm of what is negotiable in human discourse. The image of awesome power, veiled in mystery, remains.

But a vibrant, intense Christocentricity shapes Milton's theology, and in the depiction of the Son he finds an easier aesthetic challenge to negotiate. In incarnate form he constitutes the human manifestation of the Godhead, the historical Jesus who suffers and dies. Before the Incarnation and again after the Ascension he manifests himself to the world on several occasions, but he does so, in the former phase, in a mode tractable to human understanding, and in the latter, again paradoxically, as both God and man.

His relationship with Adam and Eve, however, appears somewhat less intimate than Milton's own term, 'familiar' (9.2), may suggest. We have accounts from both Adam and Eve of their own creation (these are discussed more fully in Chapter 3). The Son appears as a kindly but also awesome and indeterminate presence. Adam refers frequently to the divine entity responsible for his creation – we know it to be the Son since we know creation was his work – when he describes his earliest recollections to Raphael (this passage and the creation of Eve are discussed more fully in Chapter 3). His initial bewilderment with his own consciousness accords well with the limitations of human understanding of the Godhead:

> suddenly stood at my head a dream,
> Whose inward apparition gently moved
> My fancy to believe I yet had being,
> And lived: one came, methought, of shape divine,
> And said . . .
>
> (8.292–6)

Again, the figure reappears in a fashion Adam did not fully comprehend:

> he who was my guide
> Up hither, from among the trees appeared
> Presence divine.
>
> (8.312–14)

He recognises this figure is both awesome and worthy of adoration, but he also appreciates that he is benevolent; he speaks to him 'mildly' (8.314–17); 'the vision bright' addresses him 'with a smile' (8.367–8). Though Adam looks on the face of the Son, he seems to recall him most vividly as a presence and as a voice, 'the gracious voice divine' (8.436). Eve's experience of her own creation, as recounted to Adam, manifests a less intimate encounter with the Godhead. She recalls only a 'voice' which warned her against loving her own reflection (4.467); she felt herself 'invisibly . . . led' (4.476) to her assignation with Adam.

It is primarily as a voice that Adam and Eve perceive the Son when he comes to judge them (a role which Milton attributes to him in that at the Incarnation he will assume whatever burden he places on them now and in that he will return again at the Last Judgement to judge all of humankind). The Genesis account offers a curious and resonant phrase which shapes Milton's representation: 'They heard the voice of the Lord God walking in the garden' (3:8); in Milton's phrase, 'the voice of God they heard/Now walking in the garden' (10.97–8). In the Hebrew text, it is wholly ambiguous whether 'walking' agrees with the word for voice or the word for God. Fascinatingly, the interpretative crux attracted close discussion from the earliest Jewish commentary, *The Midrash*, through later rabbinical accounts and into Christian exegesis of the Renaissance. *The Midrash* opted for associating the walking with the voice, not with God. So, too, did many Reformed divines, though after some debate. Junius and Tremellius translated the phrase 'vocem Dei itantem', making the word for walking agree with the word voice, not the word for God. In the Authorised Version and in *Paradise Lost* the reader tends initially to perceive the agreement ambiguously, so that, in some, rather mystical, sense, the voice is walking, as though the Godhead now is distanced from mankind into one admonitory aspect of its being, the voice that warns, the voice that reproves, the voice that sentences.[20]

The Son manifests himself to Adam and Eve on a scale and in an idiom that humans may recognise and relate to as in some sense human, but he is simultaneously awesome and transcendent. Among angels, the Son manifests himself in a form that angels could relate to as in some respects angelic, but again he is awesome and transcendent. He engages in activities in the angelic idiom, hurling thunderbolts, wielding the compasses by which the created world is delimited and functioning as the head of a hierarchical system. Angels do similar things but with more difficulty and on a more modest scale (see below, chapters 2 and 4). In dealing with humankind, he sets aside associations of heavenly hierarchy and its concomitant ritual; as he comes in judgement, he advises his father:

> Attendance none shall need, nor train, where none
> Are to behold the judgment, but the judged,
> Those two . . .
>   Thus saying, from his radiant seat he rose
> Of high collateral glory: him thrones and powers,
> Princedoms, and dominations ministrant
> Accompanied *to heaven gate* . . .

> (10.80–3, 85–8, my emphasis)

That Adam had hitherto perceived the presence of the Son as awesome (though bearing likeness to human appearance and on a human scale) is reflected in his initial half-cocked response to Michael's prophecy of the Incarnation and the Atonement. In fairness, Michael's first statements invite Adam's misperception:

> [Michael] A virgin is his mother, but his sire
> The power of the most high; he shall ascend
> The throne hereditary, and bound his reign
> With earth's wide bounds, his glory with the heavens.

> [Adam]   virgin Mother, hail,
> High in the love of heaven, yet from my loins
> Thou shalt proceed, and from thy womb the Son
> Of God most high; so God with man unites,
> Needs must the serpent now his capital bruise
> Expect with mortal pain . . .

> (12.368–71, 379–84)

Michael pulls Adam down to earth by reminding him that the incarnate Son assumes all the pains and indignities that, through the Fall, humankind has become heir to, and the account of the crucifixion strikes more starkly and more paradoxically because

Adam's notion of the Son is shaped by his experience of him in his pre-incarnate form:

> For this [that is, to effect the Atonement] he shall
> > live hated, be blasphemed,
> Seized on by force, judged, and to death condemned
> A shameful and accurst, nailed to the cross
> By his own nation, slain for bringing life . . .
>
> (12.411–14)

Adam finds himself moved to a new kind of awe at the Godhead, not only at its transcendent power but at its self-sacrificing love for humankind; it is an awe focussed on the complex paradoxes and ironies of the Incarnation (the subject of Milton's second epic, *Paradise Regained*). Adam and the devout reader are left to ponder the sudden presence of the suffering Christ, the 'greater man' (1.4) effecting the restoration of Paradise through the redefined heroism of the godly martyr.

THE HOLY SPIRIT

Thus Milton depicts the Father and the Son; what of the Holy Ghost? It may be perceived as a signifying silence, but that would be a misperception, for the third component of the Trinity is pervasive within Milton's epic. Within the period 1590–1700 the term 'Holy Ghost' was commoner than its synonym 'Holy Spirit'.[21] Milton's own preferences would seem to change over his writing career. Throughout his prose work, the 'Spirit of God' and 'God's spirit' predominate, but there is a gradual shift in his preferences between 'holy ghost' and 'holy spirit' which reflects more starkly a minor shift of emphasis in the larger language community.[22] In his tracts of 1641–42 we find only the form 'holy ghost'; in 1643–45, we find nine examples of 'holy ghost' and three of 'holy spirit; in 1659–60, five examples of 'holy ghost' and seven of 'holy spirit'.[23] Quite probably there was a feeling that the word 'ghost', which had ceased to mean 'spirit' in its largest sense except in the fossilised form 'holy ghost', possessed a rather narrow, anthropomorphic connotation, as if it were a local phenomenon. Milton in his poetry uses 'holy ghost' only once, though it is in late work, *Paradise Regained* (1.139).

The spirit is the element within the Trinity by means of which the Godhead usually acts on external matter. In its most inanimate context, it transforms the globular section of chaos which the Son with golden compasses marked out for the created world:

> on the watery calm
> His brooding wings the spirit of God outspread,
> And vital virtue infused, and vital warmth.

(7.234–6; below, Chapter 4)

Milton takes the sacred text, Genesis 1:2, and asserts the potent, life-giving energy it implies.

However, the spirit functions most pervasively and, in the human context, most significantly in the inner working of the godly. When Adam is taken to view the course of human history, Eve is sedated; she wakes from her sleep as Adam returns and tells him that she has shared much of his experience, '[f]or God is also in sleep, and dreams advise' (12.611). The element that is 'in sleep', however, can best be perceived as that third component, the spirit. As such, in habit and effect, in my view it may be equated with Urania, the divine muse Milton celebrates in the invocation to Book 7:

> Standing on earth, not rapt above the pole,
> More safe I sing with mortal voice, unchanged
> To hoarse or mute, though fallen on evil days,
> On evil days though fallen, and evil tongues;
> In darkness, and with dangers compassed round,
> And solitude; yet not alone, while thou
> Visit'st my slumbers nightly, or when morn
> Purples the east: still govern thou my song,
> Urania, and fit audience find, though few.
> But drive far off the barbarous dissonance
> Of Bacchus and his revellers . . .

(7.23–33)

Early biographers confirm that Milton characteristically composed in bed, dictating the product of the night's work to his amanuensis the following morning, and on occasion, when he was late, calling out that he was aching to be milked.[24] That he perceives his poem to be distinguished by its godliness and by the holiness of its inspiration finds powerful affirmation here and elsewhere. Urania imparts her mysteries, sanctioning his song, much as God in Eve's sleep brings her truths she could not otherwise know.

Significantly, Milton sees his muse not only as an inspiration but also as a source of strength in a wholly hostile environment. Here Milton's art and Milton's personal biography touch poignantly

as, 'fallen on evil days', he senses his foes around him. 'Bacchus
and his revellers' are not difficult to identify in the 1660s; he
means the victors of the Restoration settlement and the culture
ushered in by the 'tigers of Bacchus, these new fanatics of not the
preaching but the sweating-tub' (*Readie and Easie Way to Establish a
Free Commonwealth*, second edition, *CPW*, 7, second edition, 452-3),
whom he had prophesied the end of the republic would allow once
more to dominate England. Urania makes it possible for Milton
to survive culturally, creatively, ideologically, in the 1660s. In a
similar way, the spirit of God, especially in the final books of the
epic, allows the godly to retain their integrity in the dangerous and
corrupt societies they must inhabit.

Thus, when Adam ponders the implications of Christ's Ascen-
sion, asking what will happen to those he leaves behind, Michael
answers in terms of the spirit:

> but from heaven
> He [the ascended Son] to his own a Comforter will send,
> The promise of the Father, who shall dwell
> His Spirit within them, and the law of faith
> Working through love, upon their hearts shall write,
> To guide them in all truth, and also arm
> With spiritual armour, able to resist
> Satan's assaults, and quench his fiery darts,
> What man can do against them, not afraid,
> Though to the death, against such cruelties
> With inward consolations recompensed,
> And oft supported so as shall amaze
> Their proudest persecutors . . .
>
> (12.485-97)

The passage closely interweaves Biblical reference, linking Christ's
promise of a spiritual Comforter (John 15:26) with Paul's assertion
of the primacy of justification through faith (Gal. 5:6) and his
advocacy of putting on 'the whole armour of God' (Eph. 6:10-18).
Note that Milton opposes the promptings of this 'Spirit within' to
the 'carnal laws' which some would use to bind the consciences of
the godly. Such laws have no ethical force; they are:

> laws which none shall find
> Left them enrolled, or what the Spirit within
> Shall on the heart engrave
>
> (12.522-4)

That is, these are laws either not binding or they are only binding in so far as they correspond to the inner prompting of the spirit.

The argument, carefully constructed and advanced through echoes of sacred text, enunciates principles central to the radical Protestantism of the mid-century. It asserts the primacy of individual conscience over the laws of the land, a notion which informed profoundly the political ideology of revolutionary Independency to which Milton actively subscribed. Milton's political associates of the late 1640s, military Independents of the Cromwell circle and civilians like John Bradshaw, the principal judge at Charles I's trial, acted in ways that were unsanctioned by any constitutional precedent or mandate from the political nation, but they did so in the belief that the inner spirit prompted them and sanctified their actions.[25] Indeed, at his trial in 1660, the regicide Thomas Harrison unapologetically advised his judges that, as they killed the King, 'the hearts of some have felt the terrors of that presence of God that was with his servants in those days . . . I followed not my own judgment; I did what I did, as out of conscience to the Lord,' an argument which a judge rebuked with the question, 'Will you make God the author of your treasons and murders?'[26] Milton's only objection to the question would have been in the morally loaded terminology used for what he represented as the providential establishment of a free commonwealth.

Although the inner spirit may have sanctioned the actions of the revolutionaries of 1649, at least to their own satisfaction, it assumed a defensive, rather than offensive, ideological significance in the puritan winter of the 1660s. Not only did it give strength to those regicides who met with extraordinary courage their grisly fate on the gallows and butchers' blocks of Tyburn and Charing Cross; but also it gave strength to the survivors who, like Milton and like Bunyan, continued in the faith of the godly remnant though surrounded by their enemies. It informs the doctrine of passive resistance which Bunyan enunciated to his judges at his trials for non-conformity in 1660–2, as he explains that 'the law hath provided two ways of obeying: The one to do that which I in my conscience do believe that I am bound to do, actively; and where I cannot obey actively, there I am willing to lie down, and to suffer what they shall do unto me.' It allows him to return to prison confident that he has spoken as the spirit prompted in the crises that surrounded him:

19. Kevin Sharpe, *The Personal Rule of Charles I* (New Haven, Yale University Press, 1992), 345–8.

20. Matthaeus Polus, *Synopsis Criticorum aliorumque S. Scripturae Interpretum* (London, 1669–71), 1.37; John Pearson et al., *Critici Sacri: sive Annotata Doctissimorum Virorum in Vetus ac Novum Testamentum* (1660; Amsterdam, 1698), 1.101–56; *Midrash Rabbah*, translated by H. Freedman and Maurice Simon (London: Soncino Press, 1939), 1.153. I am indebted to Gareth Lloyd Williams for his advice on the commentary tradition.

21. The electronic edition of the *Oxford English Dictionary* (hereafter *EOED2*), searched under 'holy ghost' (135 examples, 1590–1700) and 'holy spirit' (43 examples, 1590–1700). 'Spirit of God' and 'God's spirit' are also common (64 and 35 examples, 1590–1700).

22. 'Holy ghost', 78 examples 1590–1649, 57 examples 1650–1700; 'holy spirit', 22 examples 1590–1649, 21 examples 1650–1700.

23. This statement is based on the evidence of Laurence Sterne and Harold H. Kollmeier, *A Concordance to the English Prose of John Milton* (Binghamton: MRTS, 1985).

24. Helen Darbishire, (ed.) *The Early Lives of Milton* (London: Constable, 1932), p. 33; on the similarities between the reputed working practices of Milton and Virgil, see Gordon Campbell, 'Milton and the Ancients', *Journal of the Warburg and Courtauld Institutes* 47 (1984), pp. 234–8.

25. On the contradictions of Miltonic ideology, see Andrew Milner, *John Milton and the English Revolution* (London and Basingstoke: Macmillan, 1981).

26. Wedgwood, *Trial*, pp. 222–3; as we have noted, Harrison also retained a reassuring millenarian optimism.

27. John Bunyan, *A Relation of My Imprisonment*, in *Grace Abounding to the Chief of Sinners and The Pilgrim's Progress*, edited with an introduction by Roger Sharrock (London: Oxford University Press, 1966), pp. 123, 128–9.

28. N. H. Keeble, *The Literary Culture of Nonconformity in Later Seventeenth-Century England* (Leicester: University of Leicester Press, 1987).

Chapter 2

Good and Bad Angels

THE PHYSICAL PROPERTIES OF ANGELS

We have considered the bewildered glance which Adam and Eve and the readers project at Michael's cherubim massed to bar Eden to postlapsarian humankind. Angels are enigmatic creatures. Milton's era generally subscribed to the view that there were very many of them, a view which Milton shared, and yet one so rarely saw them and one knew so little about them. Certainly, in the troubled decades of the mid-century, newsbooks from time to time carried reports about angelic visitations, and major catastrophes were sometimes associated with sighting of battles in the heavens. Thus, a newsbook of 1641, reporting the current rebellion of the indigenous population in Ireland, recorded 'a prodigious Apparition in the Firmament'.[1] That account is rather uncertain about the status of the figures seen in the clouds, but another newsbook, reporting on the 'strange, and portentuous *Apparition* of two jarring Armies', witnessed fighting on the battlefield of Edgehill in the months after the battle, theorises on the status of the vision in terms of which Milton would have approved:

> . . . those legions of erring angels which fell with their great Master, *Lucifer*, are not all confined to the locall Hell, but live scattered here and there, dispersed in the empty regions of the ayre as thicke as motes in the Sunne, and those are those things which our too superstitious ancestors called Elves and Goblins, Furies, and the like.[2]

The belief that spirit wars, especially in the clouds, was a portent was ancient, as the author of *Irelands Amazement* notes (p. 3); Josephus's account of the fall of Jerusalem seems to provide the *locus classicus* (Fowler, 2.533–8n). Milton almost certainly alludes to such beliefs when he compares the fallen angels' martial games to incidents:

when to warn proud cities war appears
Waged in the troubled sky, and armies rush
To battle in the clouds.

(2.533–5)

But such events are scarcely quotidian. Yet the study of angels, what was later to be termed angelology, exercised the adepts of Milton's age as a domain of forbidden or forgotten knowledge which could, perhaps with profit, be discovered, and since they occur frequently (if enigmatically, for the most part) in sundry books of the Bible, belief in them was unsurprising in an age of faith. *Christian Doctrine* has a chapter, albeit short and tentative, on 'the Special Government of Angels' (*CPW* 6.343–50).

Milton's account of the characteristics of angels in *Paradise Lost* stresses three elements, one that is obvious (that we know very little about them and find them difficult to understand), another that is commonplace in contemporary accounts of angels (that they are very numerous), and a third which is a less common belief but which he takes pains to stress (that they are material creatures and they are governed by physical laws which relate to their materiality). I begin with the final point.

Milton's angels have weight, they may exert forces, they sleep, they eat, they excrete after a fashion, and they have sexual intercourse. Possibly, they age. Fallen ones feel pain and lose some of their sexual capacity.

Characteristically, angels travel either by flying or by walking. There are many different kinds of angels, but wings are explicitly associated with most of them. Raphael, when he visits Adam and Eve in Book 5, journeys from heaven to the gate into Paradise by flying 'with steady wing . . . then with quick fan' (5.268–9), but walks the final stretch to where Adam and Eve are having lunch. Indeed, in flight he would seem to metamorphose into a bird-like form; as he enters the part of the air where 'towering eagles' soar, 'to all the fowls he seems/A pheonix' (5.270–2), and he only returns 'to his proper shape' once he has landed (5.276–7). For whatever reason – the name is not Biblical though he figures in the apocrypha and in angelological treatises (Fowler, 5.221–3n) – Milton designates Raphael as a seraph, and as such he has a Biblical description of that 'proper shape' in Isaiah's vision of the creatures around the throne of God (Isaiah 6:2), which he follows closely, though with some glossy expansion, to produce a descriptive gem:

> six wings he wore, to shade
> His lineaments divine; the pair that clad
> Each shoulder broad, came mantling o'er his breast
> With regal ornament; the middle pair
> Girt like a starry zone his waist, and round
> Skirted his loins and thighs with downy gold
> And colours dipped in heaven; the third his feet
> Shadowed from either heel with feathered mail
> Sky-tinctured grain.
>
> (5.277–85)

His progress through fields and woods, however, would seem to be pedestrian.

Satan, too, both walks and flies. His first movement in the poem, from the fiery lake to which the Son has thrown him, is to walk, leaning on his spear, to the shore; evidently, he customarily walked in heaven, too (1.295–7). His movement from hell to earth is by means of winged flight: 'his sail-broad vans [i.e. fans or wings]/He spreads for flight' (2.927–8), though he takes something of a battering from the conflicting forces of Chaos (below, Chapter 4).

The point may seem obvious but it is an important one: angels never simply appear, as if teleported; rather, they must travel as other, terrestrial, creatures do. Indeed, at times they may move through their physical characteristic of having weight and therefore being subject to gravity. Uriel, who witnesses Satan's descent to earth from his post on the sun, travels to warn the guards of Paradise on a sunbeam, and returns back by the same route:

> Thither came Uriel, gliding through the even
> On a sun beam, swift as a shooting star
> In autumn thwarts the night.
>
> (4.555–7)

> Uriel to his charge
> Returned on that bright beam, whose point now raised
> Bore him slope downward to the sun now fallen
> Beneath the Azores.
>
> (4.589–92)

Uriel glides on a sunbeam, made possible by the fact that, before the sun falls below the equator, the end from which he departs is higher that the end at which he arrives (and vice versa, as, the sun below the horizon, he returns home). Of course, it is a rather special kind of materiality that may have its bulk thus supported.

Nevertheless, they may produce massive physical force. The task of adjusting the relationship between the earth and the sun, after the Fall, is the responsibility of 'mighty angels' (10.650) (Chapter 4).

The texture of angels allows them readily to change their form. Thus, Satan can assume the guise of 'a stripling cherub' (3.636), a term which perhaps offers, however tentatively, the notion that angels may age. 'Stripling' is an age-related category. If angels may be young, may they not also mature? Again, just as Raphael assumed the form of a phoenix, so Satan '[s]at like a cormorant' on the tree of life (4.196). He assumes a variety of animal forms in order to spy on Adam and Eve:

> he alights among the sportful herd
> Of those four-footed kinds, himself now one,
> Now other, as their shape served best his end.
>
> (4.396–8)

The force of 'like' in some of these passages may imply, not literal metamorphosis, but rather a simile; it may imply Satan is in some ways analogous to a cormorant, rather than that Satan assumes its form. But such ambiguity is dramatically excluded when Ithuriel and Zephon find him:

> Squat like a toad, close at the ear of Eve;
> Assaying by his devilish art to reach
> The organs of her fancy, and with them forge
> Illusions as he list . . .
>
> (4.800–3)

At the touch of Ithuriel's spear he resumes his own form, for 'no falsehood can endure/Touch of celestial temper, but returns / Of force to its own likeness' (4.811–13).

The loss of control over one's metamorphic capacity is certainly one of the grimmer concomitants of the angelic fall. Indeed, God annually constrains the devils in the form of serpents as a degrading and spectacular punishment for their role in the fall of humankind. The first manifestation of this is in hell as Satan on his triumphant return explains the nature of his success:

> a while he stood, expecting
> Their universal shout and high applause
> To fill his ear, when contrary he hears

On all sides, from innumerable tongues
A dismal universal hiss, the sound
Of public scorn; he wondered, but not long
Had leisure, wondering at himself now more;
His visage drawn he felt to sharp and spare,
His arms clung to his ribs, his legs entwining
Each other, till supplanted down he fell
A monstrous serpent on his belly prone,
Reluctant, but in vain, a greater power
Now ruled him, punished in the shape he sinned,
According to his doom.

(10.504–17)

The passage of which this is a part is a surprising one in a number
of ways. First, it is very long – Milton spends almost a hundred
lines describing the temporary transformation of the fallen angels
into serpents, and, while it is a descriptive *tour de force*, it seems
out of proportion to its significance within the resolution of the
epic. Moreover, it is a Miltonic invention; it is not that Milton is
investing effort in negotiating one of those exegetical cruxes which
call for a meticulous care. Again, the passage is wholly descriptive,
devoid of argument and debate. Most curiously, the fallen angels'
punishment, 'some say,' is one of a pointless annual humiliation. In
the context of Restoration politics, the most urgently felt analogy
is that strange commutation of sentence inflicted on some of the
regicides who escaped execution and who were obliged to turn up,
annually, to be carried on a hurdle to the place were they would
have been executed; or else that royalist obsession with celebrating
30 January, the date of Charles I's execution, with sermons, often
asserting that no remorse should be shown to the regicides.[3] Of
course, this passage of poetic pyrotechnics eloquently manifests
the supreme baroque artist's capacity to represent metamorphosis.
Note the treble take: Satan one moment thinks he is being hissed
when he expected praise; ponders why the other fallen angels
are hissing; then realises he is hissing too, because all have been
transformed. Milton's larger purpose, no doubt, is to rehearse at
length that point which Satan has declined fully to accept, namely,
that God's power over him is utterly transcendent. It is as it were
off the scale by which angelic power may be represented.

  While they are allowed to remain masters of their own form,
the fallen angels enjoy several benefits from their metamorphic

powers. Most singularly, it allows one building, Pandemonium, to accommodate their vast numbers, since:

> the signal given,
> Behold a wonder! they but now who seemed
> In bigness to surpass Earth's giant sons
> Now less than smallest dwarfs, in narrow room
> Throng numberless.

(1.776–80)

While one beholds a wonder, one also wonders about the moral stature of the fallen angels, and Milton's reduction is confirmed by sarcastic punning: 'Thus incorporeal spirits to smallest forms/ Reduced their shapes immense, and were at large' (1.789–90). The forms to which the fallen angels do reduce themselves, here sort of 'faerie elves' (1.781) or else Satan's disguises as cormorant and toad, manifest an indecorous self-abasement as strong as God's transformation of them into serpents in Book 10.

Satan could simply change himself into a serpent when he seduces Eve, but Milton has an exegetical obligation to make the serpent the vehicle he occupies temporarily to achieve his objective. The Genesis account says Eve was seduced by a serpent, but the commentary tradition had for long equated it with the explicitly Satanic serpent of the Book of Revelation: 'And the great dragon was cast out, that old serpent, called the Devil, and Satan, which deceiveth the whole world' (12:9). That Satan had occupied the body of the serpent (much as later devils occupy the bodies of the possessed) is the easiest exegetical route to take. As others have noted, Milton evolves a pattern of diabolic parody whereby Satan repeats depravedly the actions of the Godhead (as when, for example, we witness the infernal trinity of Satan, Sin and Death). Elsewhere in *Paradise Lost*, the word 'incarnate' is used of the incarnate Christ, a role the Son voluntarily and without reluctance accepts, in a way which defines Satan's uncertainties as squeamish and deficient in that divine humility. Thus he ponders:

> O foul descent! That I who erst contended
> With gods to sit the highest, am now constrained
> Into a beast, and mixed with bestial slime,
> This essence to incarnate and imbrute,
> That to the highth of deity aspired.

(9.163–7)

Plainly, a mind that thinks in these terms is especially susceptible to the humiliation that God inflicts on it with the annual involuntary serpentine metamorphosis.

The mixing of essences which angels do with rather less reluctance constitutes the mechanism of angelic sex. It is a matter which Milton introduces somewhat gratuitously. The notion that fallen angels have sexual intercourse with humans was commonplace. It offers one widely entertained explanation of the passage in Genesis where 'the sons of God saw the daughters of men that they were fair; and they took them wives of all which they chose' (6:2). Again, there was an ancient belief (though these categories of devil are not Biblical) that incubi (devils in the form of men) and succubi or succubae (devils in the form of women) have nocturnal coitus with, respectively, women and men. Milton alludes to the notion in *Paradise Regained* when Belial, 'after Asmodai/The fleshliest incubus,' suggests tempting the Son with attractive women, presumably succubi (*Paradise Regained*, 2.151–71).[4]

Not only do fallen angels penetrate and are penetrated by humankind; angels, or at least unfallen ones, have sexual relations with each other. Milton has Adam ferret out the information during his long conversation with Raphael. Though the sociable angel warns him off enquiring too closely into astronomy, he answers quite explicitly his questions,

> Love not the heavenly spirits, and how their love
> Express they, by looks only, or do they mix
> Irradiance, virtual or immediate touch?

> (8.615–17)

It is sometimes remarked that Raphael responds with embarrassment or that he curtails the conversation; I think his answer is much fuller than one might have expected:

> Let it suffice thee that thou know'st
> Us happy, and without love no happiness.
> Whatever pure thou in the body enjoy'st
> (And pure thou wert created) we enjoy
> In eminence, and obstacle find none
> Of membrane, joint, or limb, exclusive bars;
> Easier than air with air, if spirits embrace,
> Total they mix, union of pure with pure

Desiring; nor restrained conveyance need
As flesh to mix with flesh, or soul with soul.

(8.620–9)

'Let it suffice thee' sounds an unpromising beginning, a fobbing
off analogous to Raphael's exclusion of Adam from astronomic
knowledge (rather than speculation) (see Chapter 4). But then
Raphael does indeed tell Adam that angels embrace, and that their
embraces, unconstricted by the limitations of human physiology,
permit them to 'mix' totally.

The advancement of a view unusual in angelological tradition
serves the argument of the poem in several ways. Most certainly,
it asserts the heavenly status of sexuality, and by implication asserts
that human sexuality is not only not inherently immoral but has
about it something of the heavenly. Though angelic congress
surpasses human both qualitatively and, in sense, quantitively
(more of the bodies penetrate or are penetrated), it is still congress.
As we shall see, Milton's commitment to the paradisal, prelapsarian
status of human sexuality is both absolute and controversial (see
Chapter 3). Again, the angels, seemingly, are not gendered, so
presumably their congress is not for procreation; they do it to
express their love for each other (unless that 'stripling cherub'
has been produced by angelic coitus?) – and so, Milton argues,
do Adam and Eve; and so do all godly postlapsarian lovers. In the
repressive Christian tradition, the point is an important one. But
the passage functions centrally in Milton's account of the angels.
Once more, he asseverates that, while the physical characteristics of
angels are different from those of fallen angels, they remain *physical*;
they have a materiality (albeit specifically angelic) and are as
constrained by its physical laws as humans are by the physical laws
of our own materiality. As others have noted, the Satanic party,
whatever abilities they retain to function as succubi and incubi, are
racked by their incapacity to satisfy their profounder sexual desires.
Satan, watching the embrace of Adam and Eve, remarks:

I to hell am thrust,
Where neither joy nor love, but fierce desire
. . . with pain of longing pines.

(4.508–11)

Enforced sexual continence, far from being inherently meritorious,
is a punishment fit for the fallen angels.

Because they are material, angels require refuelling, as humans do, in order that they may perform physical actions. Simply, angels have to eat. As in the case of their sexuality, Milton's comments have about them a certain gratuitousness, and once more they stand in a minor tradition of Christian angelology. The matter is rehearsed at the beginning of Adam's conversation with Raphael. Hospitably, he has prepared an extra place for lunch (or, rather, he has had Eve prepare it – 5.313–16), but he feels an understandable diffidence about whether Raphael will be able to eat it. Raphael is very plain in his answer: 'know, whatever was created, needs/To be sustained and fed' (5.414–15). In heaven, angels eat of heavenly food, 'ambrosial fruitage' and nectar (5.427–8), but human food can also be metabolised by them:

> So down they sat,
> And to their viands fell, nor seemingly
> The angel, nor in a mist, the common gloss
> Of theologians, but with keen despatch
> Of real hunger, and concoctive heat
> To transubstantiate; what redounds, transpires
> Through spirits with ease . . .

(5.433–9)

Fowler remarks well that, 'with characteristic imaginative extremism, Milton is quite prepared to envisage angels excreting, if their corporeality entails it' (5.438–9n). Evidently they void the residual components of whatever they ingest as if by sweating. But this is a passage of committed Miltonic pugnacity. Note that he singles out 'theologians' for disputing the fact of angelic ingestion. As has been observed elsewhere, the word he uses for the process by which food is turned into energy and flesh and excrement, 'transubstantiate', reverberates with theological connotations; this is the real love feast of angel and people, and the term from the Catholic notion of that sacrament is relegated to what is going on in Raphael's digestive tract.[5]

Once we have accepted the materiality of Milton's angels and recognised that Milton is pugnaciously arguing for such characteristics, the problems which later critics have sometimes felt about the seriousness of the war in heaven largely disappear. The stuff of which angels are made is tractable to damage; it is self-healing (as the human body, less effectively, is self-healing); and some of its properties degenerate in the case of the fallen angels. As we shall see, nothing is made of nothing, and angels are capable of transforming the material of heaven into the instruments of war.

Thus, Satan both gives and receives blows, the impacts of which are analogous to the impact of human blows on mortal warriors. Abdiel sends him reeling – 'ten paces huge/He back recoiled' (6.193–4). Michael 'with huge two-handed sway' felled whole squadrons of fallen angels (6.250–1). When the fallen angels invent and manufacture artillery, the shot they fire, 'chained thunderbolts and hail of iron globes,' resembles the anti-personnel projectiles of the English Civil War, the chained shot and the like aimed at the ranks of infantry; the good angels receive its impact – 'whom they hit, none on their feet might stand' (6.592).

The good angels feel nothing keener than the embarrassment or disgrace of their overthrow. The bad angels feel pain. When Michael strikes Satan down, he recovers rapidly:

> The griding sword with discontinous wound
> Passed through him, but the ethereal substance closed
> Not long divisible, and from the gash
> A stream of nectarous humour issuing flowed
> Sanguine, such as celestial spirits may bleed,
> And all his armour stained ere while so bright.
>
> (6.329–34)

Der Mensch ist, was er isst; and so too are angels: they bleed nectarous humour because they eat nectar. Raphael lengthily explains to Adam the regenerative powers of their physiology:

> for spirits that live throughout
> Vital in every part, not as frail man
> In entrails, heart or head, liver or reins,
> Cannot but by annihilating die;
> Nor in their liquid texture mortal wound
> Receive, no more than can the fluid air:
> All heart they live, all head, all eye, all ear,
> All intellect, all sense, and as they please,
> They limb themselves, and colour, shape or size
> Assume, as likes them best, condense or rare.
>
> (6.344–53)

Some of this, though new to Adam, is already familiar to the readers; the nature of their immortality and indeed of their functional invulnerability is new to us. Of course, it prompts the question of why the good angels are engaged in this battle in the first place.

There is no reason to suppose that the angels knew anticipatively all the characteristics of angelic physiology. Satan's waging of war was presumably premissed on an assumption that a military victory of some sort could be achieved, and while the Godhead would have known otherwise the good angels engage against Satan in the belief that the conflict is purposeful. After all, their organisation is essentially military and their everyday activities, besides a fair amount of hymn-singing, seem to involve quite a bit of guarding, watching and scouting.

Moreover, the conflict is not necessarily a futile one. Satan and the fallen angels learn that their ethical corruption has brought with it a physical degeneration; they dim noticeably during the course of the events depicted in the poem. Hence the staining of Satan's armour, which implies a permanent deterioration. By the time he rouses himself from the lake of fire, he is conscious that he is 'changed in outward lustre' (1.97). When Ithuriel and Zephon discover him squat like a toad by Eve's ear, '[h]is lustre [is] visibly impaired' (4.850). Most significantly, in the war in heaven he can now feel pain for the first time, and it is horrible: he 'writhed him to and fro convolved' (6.328). As condign punishment, allowing the good angels to inflict pain on the bad makes at least as much sense as subjecting the fallen angels to endless pain in hell.

Nor is a victory for the good angels palpably impossible to them while the war continues (though the Father has secretly excluded it – 6.692). Michael certainly entertains the aspiration that Satan can be bound and 'captive dragged in chains' (6.260); of course, God later binds him satisfactorily to the lake of fire in hell, until he is released (1.210–11). So the fallen angels can be blasted, bound and made to feel pain; certainly the good angels have no reason to assume their task is anything other than purposeful and meritorious at the time at which they undertake it. Moreover, it is important in terms of their reward that they be enabled to demonstrate their courage and fidelity; they earn the Son's praise: 'Faithful hath been your warfare, and of God/Accepted, fearless in his righteous cause' (6.803–04).

The Father, however, declines to arm his angels to achieve a final victory, nor does he further incapacitate the fallen angels to impair their performance to a critical level. On the third day of the battle, the Son enters the chariot of paternal deity and overwhelms Satan's army. This is fitting in several ways. That victory comes on the third day functions typologically, anticipating the third day of the passion and Christ's victory over sin and death. Again, as Empson noticed, the fallen angels in their infernal debate misconstrue the postponement of their rout as evidence that they almost won the war in heaven. Satan's first speech in hell, to Beelzebub, offers a view of the conflict at some odds from Raphael's view and the conclusions the reader draws in Book 6:

> [I] [h]is utmost power with adverse power opposed
> In dubious battle on the plains of heaven,
> And shook his throne.
>
> (1.103–05)

Satan evidently misperceives the conflict as a close-run thing, a view untenable from the position of the godly (see chapters 1 and 6). He founds much of the heroic rhetoric of the opening books on this misperception, which in turn persuades his colleagues (and himself) that the struggle should continue.

The most telling reason for delayed divine intervention in the war in heaven is supplied by the Father, and we have no reason to suppose that Milton did not regard it as sound and adequate; this course of action best displays the Son's transcendence:

> Two days are . . . passed, the third is thine;
> For thee I have ordained it, and thus far
> Have suffered, that the glory may be thine
> Of ending this great war, since none but thou
> Can end it. Into thee such virtue and grace
> Immense I have transfused, that all may know
> In heaven and hell thy power above compare,
> And this perverse commotion governed thus,
> To manifest thee worthiest to be heir
> Of all things, to to be heir and to be king
> By sacred unction, thy deserved right.
>
> (6.699–709)

All in heaven and in hell know that the Son's power is 'beyond compare' only in the sense that they know the Father's power is also beyond compare, unavailable to his creatures as a comprehensible measure. The Son's power, like the Father's, is off the angelic scale of reckoning in the same way it is off the human.

Milton's angelology has at once convinced his readers of their immense power (compared with ours) and persuaded us that divine power massively transcends it. In the scale of being, angels are certainly above humankind, but both are so remote from the Godhead as to make those distinctions relatively trivial.

So much for the materiality and the potency of angels. What of their number? The decades following the publication of *Paradise Lost* witnessed something of a revolution in the ways in which educated Englishmen perceived the questions of population, or even the question of number. Thus in the 1680s there are concerted and quite creditable attempts by Sir William Petty and by Gregory King to address the issue of determining the population of the King's realms. Earlier, however, a vagueness which must strike us as extraordinary prevailed. To us (as to Petty) it would seem obvious that one needs a fair idea of population and its distribution to plan taxation, to estimate how much revenue this or that measure might produce. People of the mid century (and earlier) saw the issues differently, regarding them with a curious incuriousity, as though the matters could not be known or were not important. Thus, for example, John Stow's admirable *Survey of London*, first published in 1598 and reissued in revised editions, offers a wealth of information about the capital, including detailed descriptions of the topography, social and economic activity, and history of each ward of the city; but it excludes, in the latest edition available to Milton (1633), any information about the populations of those wards. Again, as one looks through contemporary accounts of battles either of the English Civil War or of the Thirty Years' War, there is often a surprising vagueness about the numbers of participants on each side.

In part, no doubt, the practical difficulties, of aggregating the data to assess population or of guessing at the numbers in the large crowd of a seventeenth-century army, may well have been a major element. But in part, I suspect, there was also a cultural redundancy about such an activity. London was easily the largest conurbation, with a population of perhaps 250,000 if the suburbs are included, out of a national total for England and Wales of about five and a half million.[6] Yet the city itself was a decidedly manageable size, as can be clearly seen from mid-century engravings like that of Wenceslas Hollar (1647). The city proper, within the wall, measured perhaps a mile and a quarter by a mile, less than twenty minutes' walk across at its widest. It could be comprehended in non-numerical terms.

This different way of regarding number profoundly shaped the representation of angels. It was an article of faith that they exist in what must have seemed to Milton huge numbers: 'I beheld till the thrones were cast down, and the Ancient of days did sit . . . A fiery stream issued and came forth from before him: thousand thousands ministered unto him, and ten thousand times ten thousand stood before him . . . ' (Daniel 7:9–10). 100,000,000 seems wildly unconscionable to someone of Milton's era; to us, it is merely one-tenth of the population of China.

Yet Milton, generally, quite potently evokes angelic profusion. There are flaccid elements, as when Adam explains to Eve that stars are useful even when he and she are asleep because '[m]illions of spiritual creatures walk the earth/Unseen' (4.677–8), which is a stark assertion of no real imaginative stimulation. But some of the most vivid descriptive passages communicate a sense of the teeming spirit world, as when we see the fallen angels '[t]hick as autumnal leaves that strew the brooks/In Vallombrosa' (1.302–03). Their first rally provokes in the reader a sense of dismay, a dismal awe at squandered potential on an inhuman scale:

> [Satan] spake: and to confirm his words, out flew
> Millions of flaming swords, drawn from the thighs
> Of mighty cherubim; the sudden blaze
> Far round illumined hell.
>
> (1.663–6)

There is a terror in so many simultaneously effecting the same action, a liberal revulsion from the militaristic reduction of individuality in this almost infinitely repeated action. Again, an alienating aspect manifests itself in Milton's analogies between angels and insects:

> As bees
> In spring time, when the sun with Taurus rides,
> Pour forth their populous youth about the hive
> In clusters . . .
> So thick the airy crowd
> Swarmed and were straitened . . .
>
> (1.768–76)

Characteristically, the view Milton encourages is one of remote amazement at an inhuman profusion. Very rarely is he numerically specific, and when he is, the effect is arresting. Thus Raphael describes the host attending the Son in the chariot of paternal deity:

> Attended with ten thousand thousand saints,
> He onward came, far off his coming shone,
> And twenty thousand (I their number heard)
> Chariots of God, half on each hand were seen . . .

(6.767–70)

Fowler has annotated this passage brilliantly, observing a distinction between the perfection of the large numbers attributed to the hosts of good angels in distinction to the innumerable multitudes of the bad angels, which in terms of Renaissance number symbolism denotes an evil plurality opposed to the goodness of the divine unity. That 20,000 puzzles briefly, till it divides, locating the Son at the symbolically dominant centre of two groups of 10,000. As Fowler remarks, large numbers generated by ten are treated as numerologically virtuous. The passage describing the Son's chariot occurs, as he notes, in the numerical centre of the poem in terms of line count (exactly so, in the first edition). The parenthetic 'I their number heard' is multi-functional. It ties Raphael's account as devised by Milton to the authority of a Biblical text (Psalms 68:17: 'The chariots of God are twenty thousand . . . the Lord is among them'). It acknowledges the simple question of psychological verisimilitude: how else may Raphael know exactly how many chariots he witnessed? And it alerts us by its intrusiveness to the point that the detail is meaningful and merits the reader's thought.

THE PROBLEM OF SATAN

Interpreting Milton's representation of Satan probably poses the major critical problem for the late-twentieth-century reader, especially if the reader is of a secular or humanistic disposition. Satan's sins seem relatively trivial both compared with his punishment and with the sins that have emerged as almost commonplace in the more grotesque aspects of our own age. His primary sin, the pride which causes him to dispute the Son's authority over him, is premissed on the recognition that there are categories of being of

a transcendent superiority. Milton acknowledges that, physically
if not spiritually, angels are superior to humankind and the
Godhead is infinitely transcendent; Satan does not acknowledge
that the Godhead as manifest in the Son is superior to the highest
rank of angels. In contrast, secular, humanistic democrats of
the late-twentieth century probably do not acknowledge the
ethical or political superiority of any creature over humankind.
Those very proper shibboleths of western democracy, universal
adult suffrage and equality before the law, value no entity above
humankind and human society. (But as we shall see, republican
Satan is also despotic Satan – below, Chapter 6; the contradiction
rests in Satanic rather than Miltonic ideology, however.)

Milton viewed the issues rather differently. It has sometimes
been perceived as paradoxical that Milton, the defender of regicide
and the English republic, should cast as his villain a figure who
would seem to embody something of the spirit of undeferential
defiance found on the roundhead side in the English revolution.
That, however, is a misperception of the nature of Miltonic
radicalism.

Milton certainly believed that Charles I and, after the restoration
of 1660, Charles II had no natural right to rule over godly
Englishmen. Inherited power on the traditional model of the
English monarchy ran counter to reason. In a spectacular after-
thought added when he issued a second edition of *Eikonoklastes*,
a refutation of Charles I's personal apologia, Milton ridicules the
notion as utterly demeaning:

> Indeed if the race of Kings were eminently the best of men, as the
> breed at *Tutburie* is of Horses, it would in some reason then be their
> part onely to command, ours always to obey. But Kings by generation
> no way excelling others, and most commonly not being the wisest or
> the worthiest by far of whom they claime to have the governing, that
> we should yeild them subjection to our own ruin, or hold of them the
> right of our common safety, and our natural freedom by meer gift, as
> when the Conduit pisses Wine at Coronations, from the superfluity
> of thir royal grace and beneficence, we may be sure was never the
> intent of God, whose ways are just and equal; never the intent of
> Nature, whose works are also regular; never of any People not wholly
> barbarous, whom prudence, or no more but human sense would have
> better guided when they first created Kings, then so to nullifie and
> tread to durt the rest of mankind, by exalting one person and his

Linage without other merit lookt after, but the meer contingencie of
a begetting, into an absolute and unaccountable dominion over them
and thir posterity

(*CPW* 3.486–7)

Thus Milton magnificently celebrates the spirit of English republi-
canism. Tutbury was famed for its draught horses; if Charles Stuart
and his offspring were inherently, in their genetic constitution,
superior to the citizens of England in their capacity to rule in
the way that Tutbury horses could pull bigger weights than other
horses, then let them rule; but they are not. Why should they
be? The mere chance of being a king's eldest surviving son only
by wild coincidence could produce the best available governor.
Citizens have a right – both divinely and by the laws of reason
and nature – to defend their own interests; it is not a privilege
to be granted by the monarch, such as when the monarch at his
coronation gave wine to be poured through the drinking-water
supply of London. The fact that James I was king and that
Charles Stuart was his eldest surviving son ought not to mean
the latter inherits power over the English people and their
property. As Milton had put it a few months earlier, 'to say,
as is usual, the King hath as good right to his Crown and
dignitie, as any man to his inheritance, is to make the Subject
no better then the Kings slave, his chattell, or his possession
that may be bought and sould' (*Tenure of Kings and Magistrates*,
CPW 3. 203).

These issues are highly pertinent for understanding the nature
of Satan's sin; it is triggered by the ceremony in which the Son,
a being previously unknown to the angels, is introduced by the
Father as his plenipotentiary. Milton describes the ritual in terms
which necessarily stimulate recollection of English coronations. In
part the reader sees the coincidence of divine and secular practice.
The word 'Messiah' derives from the Hebrew word meaning
'anointed', and the Bible explicitly speaks of God anointing Jesus
of Nazareth with the Holy Ghost (Acts 10: 38). Priests and kings
of Israel were anointed at the initiation of their office, as were
kings of England. In seventeenth-century English the term 'the
Lord's anointed' usually refers either to kings of Israel or kings of
England.[7] The celebration which follows the ceremonial announce-
ment resembles in other respects an English coronation. There is a
formal dance, the *sine qua non* of courtly celebration (5. 620–27). The

conduits do not exactly 'piss wine'; but the feast is a stately version of such libation:

> Forthwith from dance to sweet repast they turn
> Desirous; all in circles as they stood,
> Tables are set, and on a sudden piled
> With angels' food, and rubied nectar flows
> In pearl, in diamond, and massy gold,
> Fruit of delicious vines, the growth of heaven.
>
> (5.630–6)

What they drink is literally nectar, the drink of the gods, but the manner in which they drink it is redolent of more mundane celebration. They '[q]uaff' it (and thereby quaff 'immortality and joy') (5.638); the word often collocates with the names of alcoholic drinks, and nectar itself is the product of the vines of heaven, though there is no suggestion that it is fermented (see also 428). 'Nectar', contemporaneously, had some metaphoric currency as a term of praise for beer or wine.[8] Though the Father retains his own kingly role, what the angels are witnessing approximates closely to a coronation, and to the endowment of an individual with powers in some sense inherited from his father. The Father remains 'the omnipotent' (5.616), and the Son is appointed to effect 'his great vicegerent reign'; 'vicegerent', as Fowler notes, certainly had a contemporary currency as a term for the rule of kings as the Lord's anointed.[9]

After the ceremony the Son is termed 'king' and not only by the Satanic party (e.g., 5.640, 664, 690). How then can the republican Milton blame Satan for his undeferential defiance of pomp, court ceremony and the ritualisation of hierarchy? When Satan complains to Beelzebub about 'New laws from him who reigns' (5.680), he echoes the opponents of Charles I who had complained about the arbitrary imposition of what they regarded as innovative and unconstitutional legislation. Satan's speech to his followers makes a point (the Tutbury argument) we have heard already from Milton's republican writing:

> Who can in reason then or right assume
> Monarchy over such as live by right
> His equals . . . ?
>
> (5.794–6).

The revolution in heaven is perpetrated by the one-third of the angelic host who are under the command of Satan. Each is responsible for his own actions, and therefore each is as culpable as Satan. Milton uses Abdiel, not a Biblical figure, to make this point. Because Abdiel resists Satan's call to challenge the authority of the Father and the Son, it is demonstrated that any of the falling angels could have resisted; each is free to stand or fall, and it is a matter of personal choice (3.100–02). It may be felt that the point would have been even better made if there were some defections to Satan from the two-thirds of the host who are not under his command. However, Abdiel does act out the role of the solitary godly in a corrupt society, which is so much the theme of Milton's view of postlapsarian history in Books 11 and 12 (see below, Chapter 3). But Abdiel also functions as the major critic of Satan's case for opposing the Godhead. Since this issue is pivotal in the fall of the angels and since it differentiates definitively the relationship between Miltonic and Satanic republicanism, the passage merits the closest attention. Abdiel speaks to Satan and his associates:

> Canst thou with impious obloquy condemn
> The just decree of God, pronounced and sworn,
> That to his only Son by right endued
> With regal sceptre, every soul in heaven
> Shall bend the knee, and in that honour due
> Confess him rightful king? Unjust thou say'st
> Flatly unjust, to bind with laws the free,
> And equal over equals to let reign,
> One over all with unsucceeded power.
> Shalt thou give law to God, shalt thou dispute
> With him the points of liberty, who made
> Thee what thou art, and formed the powers of heaven
> Such as he pleased, and circumscribed their being?
> Yet by experience taught we know how good,
> And of our good, and of our dignity
> How provident he is, how far from thought
> To make us less, bent rather to exalt
> Our happy state under one head more near
> United. But to grant it thee unjust,
> That equal over equals monarch reign:
> Thy self though great and glorious thou dost count,
> Or all angelic nature joined in one,
> Equal to him begotten Son, by whom
> As by his Word the mighty Father made

All things, even thee, and all the spirits of heaven
By him created in their bright degrees,
Crowned them with glory, and to their glory named
Thrones, dominations, princedoms, virtues, powers,
Essential powers, not by his reign obscured,
But more illustrious made, since he the head
One of our number thus reduced becomes,
His laws our laws, all honour to him done
Returns our own. Cease then this impious rage,
And tempt not these; but hasten to appease
The incensed Father, and the incensed Son,
While pardon may be found in time besought.

(5.813–48)

Note that Abdiel concedes that, if the premise were sound, Satan's conclusion would be sound; if the Son is not superior *sui generis* to the angels (as the breed of Tutbury is superior to other breeds but much more so) then to declare him monarch over his equals would be tyranny. But since the Son is transcendent, since he has been endowed with the Father's power, and since – as Abdiel intuits – he made the angels, then his monarchy over them is not tyranny but rather an appropriate representation of their relative place in the universe.

Abdiel finds the argument when he needs it, as the godly, on Milton's account, often do, as though the holy spirit prompts them in their polemical exigencies. The hero of *Samson Agonistes* is never short of the appropriate godly rebuke when most he needs it; much later, Adam in the throes of his spiritual regeneration finds the correct next stage in his own penitent musing (see Chapter 3). In contrast, Satan stumbles from error to error. However, I rather doubt Abdiel's advice to Satan that he should repent and seek mercy. In Book 3, discussing the right doctrine of salvation, the Father explains that the fallen angels are to be excluded from the salvation which will stand open to humankind:

The first sort by their own suggestion fell,
Self-tempted, self-depraved: man falls deceived
By the other first: man therefore shall find grace,
The other none . . .

(3.129–32)

Moreover, the Father also explains (though he is talking about people who refuse the offer of salvation, rather than fallen angels),

> my long sufferance and my day of grace
> They who neglect and scorn, shall never taste;
> But hard be hardened, blind be blinded more,
> That they may stumble on, and deeper fall . . .

(3.198–201)

Just possibly Satan has not finally sinned; just possibly, he and his fellows have merely explored the possibility of sin; the rebellion in heaven has not got a very clear beginning (much as the beginning of the English Civil War is variously dated, depending on which event one regards as the crucial one). However, I think Milton expects us to see him as now sinning, and certainly his further contributions to the exchange with Abdiel have the characteristics of 'stumbling on' into an ever deeper fall.

Thus Satan disputes what Abdiel either knew formerly or more probably intuited in the heat of conflict with the ungodly, namely, that the Godhead created the angels (5.855–69). Abdiel by that stage knows that Satan's fall is irrevocable: 'I see thy fall/Determined' (5.878–79).

The whole exchange defines precisely the nature of Satan's political error – and note that for all Milton terms it 'blasphemy' Satan's offence is essentially a political one, though directed against the Godhead. Abdiel critically uses an argument which Milton in *The Readie and Easie Way to Establish a Free Commonwealth* had used in the twilight of the English republic, alongside his assertion, quoted above, that Christ left no 'vicegerent' on earth in the form of a king. It is this, that for the godly the Godhead alone has monarchic rights and powers, though in the postlapsarian world 'the kingdom of Christ our common King and Lord, is hid to this world' (*CPW*, 7, revised edition, 429). No mortal king may really know himself to be spiritually superior to his subjects (and indeed, usually, kings are not superior 'as men or Christians' to their fellows); monarchy without the superiority which is palpably manifest to the angels in the glory of the Godhead apparent in the Son is tyranny. But Satan both overvalues himself and fails to recognise the Son's eminence over him; hence Satanic republicanism is a sinful folly.

Satan is not responsible for the fall of his followers; the perseverence of Abdiel, '[t]he flaming seraph fearless, though alone/ Encompassed round with foes' (5.875–76), makes that plain. Satan's subsequent self-dedication to evil, to corrupting the earth and its inhabitants, is part of the 'stumbling on' which the Father has defined as the likeliest course of the damned. There are resonant assertions of the Satanic ethic. Once free from the sea of flame, he resolves that heroic life in the misery of hell is better than a servile life in heaven:

> Farewell happy fields
> Where joy for ever dwells: hail horrors, hail
> Infernal world, and thou profoundest hell
> Receive thy new possessor: one who brings
> A mind not to be changed by place or time.
> The mind is its own place, and in itself
> Can make a heaven of hell, a hell of heaven.
> What matter where, if I be still the same,
> And what I should be, all but less than he
> Whom thunder hath made greater? Here at least
> We shall be free . . .
>
> (1.249–59)

The sentiments undeniably have an attractive heroism. I am reminded of a poem in which the cavalier poet Richard Lovelace develops the paradox that, while the die-hard royalist is in prison for refusing to abandon his loyalty to Charles I, he enjoys a freedom he would not have if he capitulated and abandoned the cause:

> When I shall vocce aloud, how good
>   He [Charles I] is, how great should be;
> Enlarged winds that curl the flood,
>   Know no such liberty.
>
> Stone walls do not a prison make,
>   Nor iron bars a cage;
> Minds innocent and quiet take
>   That for an hermitage;
> If I have freedome in my love,
>   And in my soul am free;
> Angels alone that soar above,
>   Enjoy such liberty.[10]

Of course, Satan is less convinced than Lovelace about the 'freedom' of the angels that soar above; the community of tone and posture, however, remains.

Milton had long recognised that, in some sense, the devil has the best tunes. A beguiling heroic posture had frequently and influentially been struck by his political enemies (such as Lovelace). *Eikonoklastes*, his attack on Charles I, finds him tiptoeing around the undeniable courage the King manifested during his trial and on the scaffold. The issue had required a response in his earliest pamphlet, *Of Reformation* (1641), his attack on the role of bishops in the Church of England. The Anglican church was fiercely proud of those martyrs, like Bishops Latimer and Ridley, who had unflinchingly endured agonising executions during the period when Mary I returned England to the Catholic faith. Their deeds had become the stuff of legend; they are accessible Protestant heroes, frequently alluded to in the period 1555–1700 as examples of the achievement of the Anglican prelacy in bearing witness to the true faith. Milton argues that what they indicate is that heroism is no mark of godliness (*CPW* 1.603–04).

Milton's Satan shows courage and leadership under the most difficult of circumstances. He faces Death; he crosses alone the challenging gulf of Chaos; he offers battle to Ithuriel and Zephon and their squad of angels. He shows persistence and guile in his undercover mission to subvert the world (royalist heroism, particularly in the early 1650s, had often taken the form of undercover operations by individual agents and organisations like the Sealed Knot).[11] Milton has treated him rather differently, for example, from Pieter Breughel in his *Fall of the Rebel Angels* (1562; Musées Royaux des Beaux-Arts, Brussels), which depicts the fallen angels, immediately metamorphosed into grotesque and obscene amalgams of men, monkeys, birds, reptiles, fish and insects *as they fall*. Milton's Satan retains about him in his personality as in his physique many positive characteristics which are eroded and degraded as the poem develops.

The result is a curious duality of response to this figure. His initial sin is a political crime, an act of gross and proud misperception (it scarcely stands comparison with the death camps or terror bombing). His subsequent evil acts are all perpetrated with the Godhead's permission. He is allowed to rise from the sea of fire, he is allowed through the gates of hell, the guard withdrawn, the remaining porters his blood relatives with an interest in his escape, he is prompted to escape from Gabriel and the angels who guard Paradise by a celestial warning of divine origin. Thus he stumbles on, and in the process serves

the higher divine providence of testing humankind and providing
the necessary conditions for the transcendent sacrifice of Christ's
Atonement. As he stumbles, he retains vestiges of insight which
render his decline the more poignant. He knows his later actions
are cruel and destructive; he recognises the beauty of humankind,
creatures whom he 'could love'(4.363):

> And should I at your harmless innocence
> Melt, as I do, yet public reason just,
> Honour and empire with revenge enlarged,
> By conquering this new world, compels me now
> To do what else though damned I should abhor.
>
> (4.388–92)

The narrator, however, is rightly intolerant of those who act
against their conscience: 'So spake the fiend, and with necessity,/
The tyrant's plea, excused his devilish deeds' (4.393–4).

For certainly what we have here, nested within the divine
comedy of earth and its inhabitants, is the tragedy of Satan. In part
it narrates the fall of one from high degree to the lowest depths.
But it also ponders the sadness of lost potential and explores with
a peculiar attention to the minutiae of the character's responses the
horror of being damned.[12]

Milton, as an Arminian, took a rather more sanguine view of
human salvation than did Protestants of a Calvinist orientation.
As he has the Father explain, salvation stands open to people
who are prepared to repent; (see chapters 1 and 3). Calvinists
in general viewed humankind as consisting of a majority who
were predeterminately damned and a minority who were predeter-
minately saved; the latter, the godly, had towards the depraved
only the responsibility of controlling them. Nothing could be
done, by themselves or by others, to save those predestined to
damnation. Milton plainly distances himself from the grimness
of that doctrine. But the Father makes clear that saving grace
is available to none of the fallen angels. Certainly, Satan feels
no inner promptings of grace to suggest he may eventually find
salvation, and he grimly (and correctly) concludes that there is no
hope for him and his fellows, though his reasoning is wrong. He is
not excluded from salvation because he is incapable of submission
(4.81); he is incapable of submission because he is excluded from
salvation.

So the reader observes this glittering creature, still distinguished by many of the God-given properties appropriate to his high angelic status, gradually corrupted until finally and spectacularly he is metamorphosed into an absurd but monstrous snake. What that long and lingering account of the degradation of the fallen angels does is define the benevolence of the Godhead's treatment of humankind. The passage follows hard on the qualified and not wholly unkindly judgement passed on Adam and Eve – the Son pities them and clothes their nakedness – and it is followed in Books 11 and 12 by the ultimate vision of the salvation of the godly through the Atonement. The Father's differentiation in Book 3 between the treatment of humankind and the treatment of the fallen angels is abstract and schematic; the concluding books act out what it means experientially. For godly humans, there is (after suffering) a glorious promise of redemption, which is made the more remarkable by the reader's sense of how it differs from the anguish of the unredeemable fallen angels (whose fate will be shared by ungodly humans). Godly humankind's fate is a sad and grim one, but it could have been much more frightful. Adam and Eve and their offspring could all share Satan's fate; some, who pray and repent and persevere, will escape it. The tragedy of Satan makes that divine comedy seem the more remarkable and fortunate.

NOTES

1. Anon., *Irelands Amazement, Or the Heavens Armado* (London, 1641), sig. A2v.

2. Anon., *A Great Wonder in Heaven, shewing the late Apparitions seen on Edge-Hill* (London, 1641), p. 3.

3. Wedgwood, *Trial*, p. 219; *The Diary of John Evelyn* (1907; London and New York: J. M. Dent and E. P. Dutton, 1945), 1.349–50, 2.132, pp. 273, 293; Peter J. Kitson advises me that the custom of sermons to commemorate the execution of the King continued to flourish in the 1790s.

4. Carey notes that Milton elsewhere favours the alternative interpretation of the Genesis passage, adopting it in *Paradise Lost* 11.573–87 (*Paradise Regained* 2.178–81n); however, Edward E. Ericson Jr explains the inconsistency as Milton's recognition of the equal status of the alternative exegetical strategies in 'The Sons of God in *Paradise Lost* and *Paradise Regained*', *Milton Quarterly*, 25 (1991), pp. 79–89.

5. Thomas N. Corns, *Milton's Language* (Oxford: Blackwell, 1990), p. 106; John Milton, *Complete English Poems, Of Education, Areopagitica*, edited by Gordon Campbell (London and Vermont: Dent and Tuttle, 1993) (hereafter Campbell), 5.434–38n.

6. Sir George Clark, *The Later Stuarts 1660–1714*, second edition (Oxford: Clarendon Press, 1955), pp. 38–40.

7. Based on the 12 examples of the phrase found in *EOED2*.

8. *EOED2*, searched on 'nectar' and 'quaff'.

9. See *EOED2*, s.v. 'vicegerent'. Milton uses it variously; sometimes to refer to the civil magistrate (as in his assertion in an early tract that the magistrate 'ought to be obey'd as [God's] vicegerent' – *CPW*, 1.771); once later to assert that none may act as God's plenipotentiary on earth ('All Protestants hold that Christ in his church hath left no vicegerent of his power, but himself without deputie, is the only head therof' *CPW*, 7.429).

10. Richard Lovelace, 'To Althea, From Prison', lines 21–32, in *Selected Poems*, edited by Gerald Hammond (Manchester: Fyfield, 1987).

11. David E. Underdown, *Royalist Conspiracy in England 1649–1660* (New Haven: Yale University Press, 1960), passim.

12. John Stachniewski, *The Persecutory Imagination: English Puritanism and the Literature of Relgious Despair* (Oxford: Clarendon Press, 1991), especially Chapter 8.

Chapter 3

People

Unlike the account in Genesis, which is utterly enigmatic about the personalities and motivations of Adam and Eve, *Paradise Lost* offers as intimate an interior view of the protagonists' mental process as a Shakespearean tragedy; sometimes this occurs through the dramatic mechanism of soliloquy in which characters in some sense speak their thoughts or are depicted in lamentation, but more often it is expressed through dialogue or through exchanges in which characters recount recollection of their thoughts, feelings and perceptions.

The problem Milton engages, especially in depicting the first few hours of the lives of Adam and Eve, is a uniquely challenging one. Imagine the sensibility of an accomplished human adult who knows nothing or almost nothing. In the development of the human infant, the most obvious analogue available to Milton in his own experience, the neonate learns to interpret phenomena seemingly simultaneously with the ability to name them; the child, however, is not perceived as wholly rational. The processes are interactive and incremental. Adam, on his creation, has the perceptions and the appetites of an adult male; he has a powerful intellect, perfect as no postlapsarian human intellect (save that of the incarnate Christ) has been perfect, and it actively seeks out and interprets the sense data it receives. Perhaps he can best be thought of as if he were a deeply traumatised genius in whom amnesia has taken away not only all knowledge and recollection but also the confidence that he can know the names of things.

The early consciousness of Adam constitutes the subject of part of his conversation with Raphael in Book 8. (Raphael, having missed witnessing that component of the creation, has asked for

Adam's account.) Milton begins with a pre-emptive assertion of
the difficulty of the task; he has Adam remark, 'For man to tell
how human life began/Is hard; for who himself beginning knew?'
(8.250–51). In a sense Adam accepts the task of describing his own
birth. On recollection, it is initially a material rather than a spiritual
process, but one which he can only represent and make sense of in
terms of subsequent experience:

> As new waked from soundest sleep
> Soft on the flowery herb I found me laid
> In balmy sweat, which with his beams the sun
> Soon dried . . .

> (8.253–6)

Of course, Adam at that point did not know what sleep was like,
and indeed, when he first falls asleep (8.287–91), as he recollects,
he thinks he is returning into the state of non-being before his
creation. But note how the creation shares some similarities with
aspects of the normal birthing process; it is explicitly a damp and
exhausting experience (though there are also points of analogy
in Milton's account with the emergence of a butterfly from its
chrysalis).

Adam has certain innate instincts: '[b]y quick instinctive motion'
(8.259) he springs up. He knows how to walk and to run, much as
some subhuman creatures do, and he makes an inventory of his
body and learns what its parts are capable of. He also discovers
that he has been created with knowledge of the names of things.
That capacity, which in Genesis is not disclosed till he names
the animals (Genesis 2:19–20), is present in this account from the
beginning:

> to speak I tried, and forthwith spake,
> My tongue obeyed and readily could name
> What e'er I saw. Thou sun, said I . . .

> (8.271–3)

But he cannot name himself nor explain his origins or purpose
(8.270–1). Nor does he know the characteristics of the objects he
names; indeed, he asks the sun, hills, dales, and the like, for
information about his own creation and his own creator. Yet,
though he is created without knowledge of the Godhead, he
nevertheless recognises in himself a spiritual impulse towards praise
of his creator, and the feeling is profounder than knowledge:

> Tell me, how I may know him, how adore,
> From whom I have that thus I move and live,
> And feel that I am happier than I know.

(8.280–2)

The non-human cannot, of course, vouchsafe the required infor-
mation; Adam did not know this, but the learning curve he is on
is a steep one. More significantly, the lines assert the primacy of
spiritual feeling over spiritual knowledge. He wanders 'I *knew* not
whither' (8.283, my emphasis), and fatigued he sleeps. In sleep comes
a divinely inspired dream which tells him his name and his role both
as father of his race and lord of Paradise. Adam never really focusses
on the Godhead, never views him with particularity. In his dream,
he is 'one . . . of shape divine' (8.295); he wakes to find a 'Presence
divine' (8.314), 'the heavenly vision' (8.356), 'the vision bright' (8.367),
'the gracious voice' (8.436). We know him to have been the Son
(Chapter 1, above), but the newly created Adam is ignorant about the
constitution of the Godhead (though he learns it, if he did not already
know, from Raphael in his account of the war in heaven, which
has preceded his own account of his creation, and he could have
concluded thus in the light of what Raphael had said about creation).

Adam's first conversation with the Son proves demanding; he
remarks that he was 'strained to the highth/In that celestial colloquy
sublime' (8.454–5). He emerges from it knowing much more. Some
information is transmitted rapidly and without verbalisation; with
'sudden apprehension' (8.354) he knows the nature of the beasts that
the Son brings him to name. The most important lesson, however,
is gravely explicit, as the Son explains the nature of the trial which
has been placed at the heart of Paradise in the form of 'the tree whose
operation brings/Knowledge of good and ill' (8.323–4). It is the only
imperative communicated to him in this dialogue:

> for *know*,
> The day thou eat'st thereof, my sole command
> Transgressed, inevitably thou shalt die;
> From that day mortal, and this happy state
> Shalt loose, expelled from hence into a world
> Of woe and sorrow.

(8.328–33, my emphasis)

Can this be fair, given that Adam is asked to interpret an imperative
which incorporates new categories like 'death' and 'woe'? The issue

of such fairness is pivotal to the thesis of the poem, and note how skilfully Milton has negotiated it. Adam does indeed *know* happiness and the pleasure of living in Paradise, and Milton has established that a category may be known by its opposite. Thus, in being, Adam may be said to know non-being, the state which preceded being and which preceded consciousness. His happiness is persistently stressed; he may fairly be assumed to understand the concept of unhappiness, of 'woe'.

In the hours and days which follow Adam's potent rationalism works impressively on his perceptions both of his own characteristics and of the created world. God plays an amusing game with him, though as others have remarked with chilling anticipation of the final test; when Adam, perceiving that all other species having been created in pairs, notices his own solitariness and asks for remedy, he tells him that he is surrounded by animals with which to '[f]ind pastime' (8.375). Adam resists the suggestion, holding out for the creation of a fit companion. God, admitting that his argument had been advanced merely 'for trial only' (8.447), concludes:

> [I] find thee knowing not of beasts alone,
> Which thou hast rightly named, but of thy self . . .
>
> (8.438–9)

Adam has recognised in himself an impulse towards pairing off, and he appreciates that an element of the divine spirit within him precludes too close an intimacy with lower animals, though it is the Son, not Adam, that gives this spirit a name (8.440). (Incidentally his recognition that each creature behaves according to its own nature, if Eve were to know it as well as Adam, would arouse certain suspicions about the intimate approaches of talking serpents.) Adam receives no instruction in how to respond to Eve: as in the Genesis account, he names her and asseverates the nature of the marital bond (8.494–9). He feels at once an accession of joy, and she too 'what was honour knew' (8.508). Both sexual appetite and the sense of its sanctification in the decorum and institution of marriage are apparently innate.

Adam continues to learn a great deal. Some things, like the war in heaven and the associated insights into the nature of the Godhead, are a matter of instruction. God makes him know these things because it is only fair that he should know them. In that

frequently quoted and unflinching phrase from the Argument to
Book 5, 'God to render man inexcusable sends Raphael to admonish
him of his obedience, of his free estate, of his enemy near at hand;
who he is, and why his enemy, and whatever else may avail Adam to
know.' Again, to make the experience of postlapsarian life endurable,
he is vouchsafed knowledge of what is to come, of the suffering and
the eventual triumphs which are the subject of those visions Adam
witnesses in Books 11 and 12. But technically more demanding for
Milton's powers of exposition are those elements of knowledge he
arrives at through his own investigation.

The fullest example is his discussion with Eve of the nature of
dreams. After she wakes on the morning after Satan's entry into
Paradise, troubled by the evil dream she has inspired, she turns
to Adam for explanation, provided in terms of the capacities of
the human mind, which would seem to be arrived at through
his meditation on the workings of his own mind (5.95–115). He
postulates the problem, 'Yet evil whence? In thee can harbour
none,/Created pure' (5.99–100). He offers a detailed account of the
origins of dreams (imagination, which functions purposefully and
creatively when it serves reason, grinds away on its own when
reason sleeps, producing mismatched images from disjointed recol-
lections). Though the psychology is, in contemporary terms,
sound, his conclusion leaves some of the dream unexplained; he
can identify most of it in the previous night's conversation, 'But
with addition strange' (5.116). Pure reason has its limitations in the
war against the great deceiver.

So far we have considered only what may be termed useful
knowledge, things that Adam and Eve need to know so that
they can be fairly tested, things they need to know to live in
Paradise, and things they need to know to establish the tradition
of true belief and prophecy which they bequeath to their heirs
to enable the godly thereafter to negotiate life after the Fall. But
Adam and Eve and their heirs may enjoy non-useful knowledge
or what is sometimes nowadays termed useless information. In a
sense, Raphael had disclosed an angelic interest in such information
when he asked Adam to recount his experience of the creation of
himself and of Eve. As we have seen (Chapter 2), Adam concludes
his account by pressing Raphael for information about the angelic
experience of physical love.

This is information that Adam and Eve do not need to know.

Some information is, in a sense, trivial in that it has no bearing on the important decisions which Adam and Eve are to face. Some scientific speculation, Milton suggests, probably remains outside the scope of human enquiry, or at least may not be advanced beyond hypothesis to certain knowledge. The paradigmatic case is constituted by the central questions engaging seventeenth-century astronomy. Since Adam has in his company a space traveller who has seen with his own eyes how earth relates to the planets and stars, he understandably frames to him the questions which his own observations, ordered by his reason, have determined to be cardinal (they are the same questions which by Milton's time had interested astronomers for a century or more). He is, as the Argument puts it, 'doubtfully answered', and reminded by Raphael that he has been told quite a bit about heaven already. The information that he seeks is not pertinent to his condition: 'Solicit not thy thoughts with matters hid,/Leave them to God above, him serve and fear' (8.167–8), a point which Adam accepts:

> But apt the mind or fancy is to rove
> Unchecked, and of her roving is no end;
> Till warned, or by experience taught, she learn,
> That not to know at large of things remote
> From use, obscure and subtle, but to know
> That which before us lies in daily life,
> Is the prime wisdom, what is more, is fume,
> Or emptiness, or fond impertinence,
> And renders us in things that most concern
> Unpractised, unprepared, and still to seek.
>
> (8.188–97)

As others have done, I find the passage fascinating. A strong philistine streak runs through militant puritanism. It finds a cultural manifestation in the sanctioned iconoclasm of the 1640s. Marvell, perhaps poignantly, represented the cultural revaluation in his 'Horatian Ode on Cromwell's Return from Ireland' through the image of 'forward youth' who must set aside 'his numbers languishing' and assume an active, uncultured and militant role. Milton returns quite frequently to the relative value of the life of the mind. In his prose works he stresses that uneducated religious activists outside the pale of formal religion had the capacity to arrive at those central truths necessary for the informed choices on which their salvation depends (for example, in *The Likeliest*

Means to Remove Hirelings out of the Church, *CPW*, 7, revised edition, 302). In his later brief epic, *Paradise Regained*, in a passage which has provoked much special pleading, Milton has the Son dismiss Satan's temptation to revel in the learning and culture of the classical world with:

> who reads
> Incessantly, and to his reading brings not
> A spirit and judgment equal or superior, .
> (And what he brings, what needs he elsewhere seek)
> Uncertain and unsettled still remains,
> Deep-versed in books and shallow in himself,
> Crude and intoxicate, collecting toys,
> And trifles for choice matter, worth a sponge;
> As children gathering pebbles on the shore.

> (*Paradise Regained*, 4.322–30)

The Son speaks specifically of classical learning; the distinction between that and the fruits of scientific speculation would have been less keenly felt in the seventeenth century, especially among those who, like Milton, had some experience of the interests, enthusiasms and ethos of Italian academies. The pivotal issue in the Son's response is that 'spirit and judgement' reside in the interiority of the godly and are not to be arrived at speculatively.

That the mind may wander, that it may pursue that which is interesting over that which is necessary, is expressly a prelapsarian trait; Adam has arrived at the conclusion through considering the activities of his own unfallen mind, albeit prompted by Raphael's rebuff. Its dangers, though, are not understated. That cluster of words, 'wandering thoughts . . . of her roving is not end', prompts recollection of the first meeting of speculative virtuosi among the fallen angels in hell, as they while away time till Satan returns[1]:

> Others apart sat on a hill retired,
> In thoughts more elevate, and reasoned high
> Of providence, foreknowledge, will and fate,
> Fixed fate, free will, foreknowledge absolute,
> And found no end, in wandering mazes lost.

> (2.557–61)

A notion of puritan self-abnegation lies behind both the response of the Son, that of Adam, and Marvell's own paradigm. In a poetry of great depth of cultural allusion and, particularly in Milton's case, in a poetry richly informed by an awareness of currently problematic issues of speculative science, they subordinate those achievements to starker imperatives. Knowing what is not useful is much inferior to doing what is right, and unrestrained pursuit of 'impertinent' knowledge may disguise that simple truth. The passage anatomises the ideological crisis of the puritan poet, invoking a profound range of cultural experience in defence of a creed which has, at its core, a great simplicity. In the context of the thesis of the poem, however, the passage works to prepare the way for establishing the fairness of, most specifically, the fall of Eve, for it acknowledges that intellectual challenge, with its own essential excitement, is as nothing compared with plain obedience to the Godhead.

Adam's primary source of information about the working of the human mind is his observation and thinking about his own mind, a process which rapidly produces considerable advances in his knowledge. That alone would have been enough to demonstrate to him that, while certain impulses (primarily the impulse to worship God and the impulse to love Eve) are innate and some information is arrived at by special procedures (such as the sudden accession of knowledge about the creatures he names) the human mind characteristically works not through intuition but through a reasoning process in which the stages may be made explicit. Moreover, Raphael, pressed on the nature of angelic life and its relationship to the rest of God's creations, differentiates it from human in terms of the primary mode of its rational process. Angels and people consume nourishment, taking from it:

> both life and sense,
> Fancy and understanding, whence the soul
> Reason receives, and reason is her being,
> Discursive, or intuitive; discourse
> Is oftest yours, the latter most is ours,
> Differing but in degree, of kind the same.
>
> (5.485–90)

Generally, human reason is expected to arrive at its conclusions by proceeding logically from stated premises; angels more often simply arrive intuitively at conclusions. That is not to say that people are incapable of intuition (or angels of discursive reason), but when people intuit they should do so guardedly, with a sense that this constitutes deviation from their more usual practice. Knowing himself, Adam already knows that, but the explicit rehearsal of it by his angelic counsellor renders it even more inexcusable when, as we shall see, his intuition prompts him to fall.

THE PRIVATE LIFE OF ADAM AND EVE

Adam innately knows he would like to sleep with the first woman he sees; Eve's own appetites curiously concur. This forms the subject of the perhaps surprising account which Eve gives Adam (and indirectly both the reader and Satan, who, disguised as a decidedly postlapsarian tiger, stalks them as if they were 'two gentle fawns at play' – 4.404). She is describing her earliest recollections of consciousness. She awoke feeling uncertainties analogous to those of the newly created Adam, wondering 'what I was, whence thither brought, and how' (4.452). Prompted by the sound of running water, she finds a '[s]mooth lake' (4.459). Such is her level of ignorance, she confuses the reflection of the sky with the sky itself; more interestingly, she mistakes her own reflection for another person, towards whom she feels the stirrings of sexual appetite. She would have 'pined with vain desire' had not 'a voice . . . warned' her, explaining the physical properties of reflections, and, much more significantly, establishing the notion of gender and her relation to the 'he' to whom she is to be introduced and who now 'stays/Thy coming, and thy soft embraces' (4.465–471).

The issues are complex. Note that, like Adam, Eve even on reflection has only a vague comprehension of the Godhead, the mysterious 'voice'. The collocation of 'voice' and 'warning' prompts recollection of the opening line of Book 4 ('O for that warning voice . . . '). The voice warns her against the folly of neonatal ignorance; it will not warn her again in quite such straightforward terms. Adam, too, had contemplated the society of inappropriate objects of desire when he had turned from the bestial herd to ask the Godhead for a fitting mate. Eve, however, does not make her own mind up. Though, superficially, the course she contemplates is narcissism, the profounder impulse she feels is towards love of her own gender. Certainly, when she sees Adam, her first impulse is at the least reluctance:

I espied thee, fair indeed and tall,
Under a platan, yet methought less fair,
Less winning soft, less amiably mild,
Than that smooth watery image; back I turned . . .

(4.477–80)

Adam knew what he wanted; Eve is twice told what she must
have, first by the warning voice and then by Adam:

Return fair Eve,
Whom fly'st thou? Whom thou fly'st, of him thou art,
His flesh, his bone; to give thee being I lent
Out of my side to thee, nearest my heart
Substantial life, to have thee by my side
Henceforth an individual solace dear;
Part of my soul I seek thee, and thee claim
My other half . . .

(4.481–8)

Adam's account to Raphael of the creation of Eve makes two
points quite clearly: the mode of her creation is not of Adam's
election (the Godhead does not ask him if he would like to donate
a rib), and it causes him neither pain nor even discomfort. It occurs
in a sort of waking dream (8.452–80). There is no suggestion that he
is in any sense weakened or rendered imperfect by the process. Yet
it is the basis of the property right which he claims over her. His
initial comments engage, not what he may offer Eve, but what
Eve owes and must offer him, 'an individual solace'. 'Solace', in
Milton's time, could have meant either an alleviation of suffering
or else that which gives delight or pleasure; 'individual' could mean
'inseparable', but it also meant 'peculiar to a singular person'.

Milton, in the starkly masculinist and patriarchal version he
gives of the marriage of Adam and Eve, effectively demystifies
gender relations both as they were understood in his own age
and as his contemporaries perceived them to be inscribed in
Biblical doctrine. Their story unfolds as a story of profound,
tragic but redeeming love, but in place of the Petrarchan and
sub-Petrarchan roles available to Milton as a pattern for Adam,
he observes instead a politically uncluttered paradigm. Adam's
courtship involves neither reverence nor servitude nor frustration.
It follows a rather conservative pattern of a patriarchally arranged
marriage in which the bride is passed by her father (and master)

to her husband (and master). The Godhead acts the father's role. He orders her to stop pining for the female image of herself but to follow him to Adam, to whom 'thou . . . shalt bear/Multitudes like thyself, and thence be called/Mother of the human race'; she does not perceive herself to have an alternative: 'what could I do,/But follow straight' (4.472–6).

It is hard to see anything elective in this process. Further, though she accedes to Adam, he is not the most attractive creature she has seen, and she does so with some distinct reluctance:

> thy gentle hand
> Seized mine, I yielded, and from that time see
> How beauty is excelled by manly grace
> And wisdom, which alone is truly fair.
>
> (4.488–91)

Though the hand is 'gentle', seizing and yielding nevertheless imply assault; that Milton has her respond thereafter makes the passage more, rather than less, disturbing. She also learns to value essential masculinity over her perception of what constitutes the feminine. No wonder Adam '[s]miled with superior love' at her 'submissive charms' (4.498–9). Book 4 gives us Eve's version of events, a version she speaks to Adam; in Book 8, in a discussion between Adam and Raphael which occurs chronologically as well as narratively after the conversation of Book 4, we have Adam's account. 'Nature,' on Adam's account, made her respond retiringly to his approach – 'seeing me, she turned;/I followed' (8.507–8). The accelerated courtship in Adam's recollection seems more verbalised than in Eve's; she succumbs to his 'pleaded reason' (8.510).

Marriage rapidly follows the courtship. Milton takes pains to emphasise that their relationship is fully paradigmatic of wedded love in his own world. Adam leads her to 'the nuptial bower' (8.510) in a ceremony redolent of the bedding of the bride in early modern England; earth, 'each hill', gales and airs act as wedding guests; indeed, the last fling odours, much as human wedding guests might sprinkle the marriage bed with petals. The evening star carries the bridal lamp, while the nightingale sings a marriage hymn (8.511–20).

Biblical commentators had long pondered over the nature of prelapsarian sexuality. Outside the pale of Christian respectability, a pagan myth of the golden age retained a libertine usefulness.

Among Milton's more secular contemporaries, it received occasional celebration as the imagined site of sexual freedom in a world dominated by Christian constraint. Thus, Lovelace entertains reveries about a time when

Lasses like autumn plums did drop,
And lads, indifferently did crop
        A flower, and a maidenhead.

Then unconfined each did tipple
Wine from the bunch, milk from the nipple.
        Paps tractable as udders were
Then equally the wholesome jellies,
Were squeezed from olive-trees, and bellies,
        Nor suits of trespass did fear.[2]

Such pagan fantasy posed the dark obverse of the dominant view among Christian commentators; namely, that in Eden Adam and Eve, though they had the potential for intercourse, did not consummate their relationship. Postlapsarian sexuality was generally perceived as a sinful business consequent on the fall or a kind of comfort unnecessary before it. Those commentators who did accept prelapsarian coitus thought it qualitatively (and technically) distinct from its fallen manifestation: specifically, male arousal was deemed to be within Adam's choice or election, rather than the subject of more unpredictable promptings, as in the fallen world.[3]

Milton's representation of sexuality in Eden (and in the fallen world) observes no simple dichotomies (godly before the fall, tainted thereafter). Certainly, the first coitus after the fall manifests Adam and Eve's sinful condition (it is also the first action they think to do). Unlike their prelapsarian coitus, it is performed outdoors (the 'verdant roof' of trees above them – 9.1038 – serves only to promote recollection of the privacy of their bower, now abandoned). Their motivation is '[c]arnal desire' (9.1013); their passion resembles inebriation with 'new wine' (9.1008), and they wake from their post-coital nap somewhat hung over – 'up they rose / As from unrest' (9.1051–2).

Milton perhaps glances at the notion that sex is a postlapsarian gift to make life in the fallen world tolerable when, in a complex and ironic phrase, he speaks of that first coitus after the fall as the 'solace of their sin' (not only solace in their sinfulness but solace originating in the sinfulness). But, in a passage of great vigour and

technical accomplishment, he has already argued that reciprocated
sexual love within marriage, even in the fallen world, can share the
characteristics of Edenic sexuality.

At the end of the day depicted in Book 4, Adam and Eve
retire to their bower. Milton encourages the assumption that coitus
habitually concludes their days together:

> nor turned I ween
> Adam from his fair spouse, nor Eve the rites
> Mysterious of connubial love refused.

(4.741–3)

That parenthetic 'I ween,' that is, 'I surmise,' alerts the reader
that this is a Miltonic belief with which some would take issue.
But Milton takes issue first. He digresses from the topic of what
Adam and Eve are up to in bed (thus performing a turning away,
an averting of the intrusive gaze, appropriate to the privacy which
characterises prelapsarian sex), rounding on those who would
argue that sex had no place in Paradise:

> Our maker bids increase, who bids abstain
> But our destroyer, foe to God and man?
> Hail wedded love, mysterious law, true source
> Of human offspring, sole propriety
> In Paradise of all things common else.
> By thee adulterous lust was driven from men
> Among the bestial herds to range, by thee
> Founded in reason, loyal, just, and pure,
> Relations dear, and all the charities
> Of father, son, and brother first were known.
> Far be it, that I should write thee sin or blame,
> Or think thee unbefitting holiest place,
> Perpetual fountain of domestic sweets,
> Whose bed is undefiled and chaste pronounced,
> Present, or past, as saints and patriarchs used.
> Here Love his golden shafts employs, here lights
> His constant lamp, and waves his purple wings,
> Reigns here and revels; not in the bought smile
> Of harlots, loveless, joyless, unendeared,
> Casual fruition, nor in court amours
> Mixed dance, or wanton mask, or midnight ball,
> Or serenade, which the starved lover sings
> To his proud fair, best quitted with disdain.

(4.748–70)

Milton's advocacy of wedded chastity, of the sanctification of sexuality in the institution of marriage, finds ample confirmation in the protestant tradition. But note especially the way in which he pugnaciously links Edenic sexuality to the contemporary world. 'Who bids abstain?' has the obvious immediate answer, 'The Church of Rome,' with its elevated view of virginity and the celibacy of those in holy orders; Milton leaves the reader to make the equation of the Pope with 'our destroyer' (who is also equatable with Satan).

The bedrooms of the godly share common ground with the bower of prelapsarian Adam and Eve, but they are distinct from the world of Restoration depravity. 'Mixed dance,' etc., carries a powerful charge in seventeenth-century cultural politics; old puritan values, which opposed the practices of the court of Charles I in the 1630s, are reinvigorated in the 1660s with regard to the much more scandalous court of Charles II (see below, Chapter 6). Milton also works to distinguish godly love poetry from the received tradition. That Petrarchan cult in which the lover, rebuffed by his mistress, persists in his adoration of her, is explicitly dismissed; both she and the whole fantasy of courtly love are 'best quitted with disdain'. The robustness of Adam's courtship technique evidently retains its validity in Milton's view.

Though Adam and Eve, once they have fallen, participate in an ungodly sexual act, the true solace of wedded love will be available to them once they are regenerate.

Note the gendering of the most valued relationships which have their origins in married love – father, son, brother. That is juxtaposed interestingly with the gender politics implied in the rejection of Petrarchanism. Again, Milton demystifies the nature of the power relationship between the sexes, declining to obscure in literary terms the quotidian experience of husband and wife in his own age.

Adam persistently speaks respectfully to Eve. His address characteristically is decorous and formal: '[s]ole partner and sole part of all these joys' (4.411); '[f]air consort' (4.610); '[d]aughter of God and man, accomplished Eve' (4.660); '[b]est image of my self and dearer half' (5.95); and so on. He undertakes to report to her whatever information he comes by which she should know. Thus, when Michael in Books 11 and 12 vouchsafes to him a vision of futurity, Eve simultaneously receives a vaguer message in a drugged sleep

(11.367) from which she receives a generally propitious account
(12.610–15) though not the definitive prophetic utterance, which must
be delivered to her by Adam in due course:

> go, waken Eve;
> Her also I with gentle dreams have calmed
> Portending good, and all her spirits composed
> To meek submission: thou at due season fit
> Let her with thee partake what thou hast heard,
> Chiefly what may concern her faith to know . . .
>
>   (12.594–9)

Note that it is left to Adam's judgement what and when Eve
should be informed; 'chiefly' implies selection. The dreams have
also engendered a new spirit of 'meek submission,' presumably as
well to her husband as to the Godhead and her due punishment.

A division of roles and responsibilities obtains which habitually
has Adam talking to those of rank above them and Eve retiring.
When Raphael calls, Adam sees him coming 'as in the door he
sat/Of his cool bower'; Eve is 'within', preparing a meal (5.299–307),
though Adam calls her out to watch Raphael's arrival (and to tell
her to prepare more food for their guest) (5.308–20). Eve eventually
slips away from the dialogue between Adam and Raphael when
the former gets on to the topic of astronomy:

> So spake our sire, and by his countenance seemed
> Entering on studious thoughts abstruse, which Eve
> Perceiving where she sat retired in sight,
> With lowliness majestic from her seat,
> And grace that won who saw to wish her stay,
> Rose, and went forth among her fruits and flowers,
> To visit how they prospered, bud and bloom,
> Her nursery; they at her coming sprung
> And touched by her fair tendance gladlier grew.
> Yet went she not, as not with such discourse
> Delighted, or not capable her ear
> Of what was high: such pleasure she reserved,
> Adam relating, she sole auditress;
> Her husband the relater she preferred . . .
>
>   (8.39–52)

The division of roles is perhaps greater than it initially seems;
while 'nursery' primarily means a place in which young plants are

brought on, it probably carries a secondary suggestion, anticipating Eve's role as mother of mankind, of the place where children are reared. Certainly, the flowers are curiously personified, like children noticing their mothers' presence and responding by growing 'gladlier'. Milton has Eve prepare food and check on the nursery while Adam discusses speculative science with the angel (though he also suggests that, while Adam's discourse on astronomy is futile over-reaching, Eve's activities are purposeful and associated with a general notion of fertility).

Milton explicitly and persistently reiterates the inequality of Adam and Eve. Satan, trying to make sense of his first view of them, remarks on their physical disparity and draws a conclusion with which Milton, presumably, concurs:

> For contemplation he and valour formed,
> For softness she and sweet attractive grace,
> He for God only, she for God in him:
> His fair large front and eye sublime declared
> Absolute rule; and hyacinthine locks
> Round from his parted forelock manly hung
> Clustering, but not beneath his shoulders broad:
> She as a veil down to the slender waist
> Her unadorned golden tresses wore
> Dishevelled, but in wanton ringlets waved
> As the vine curls her tendrils, which implied
> Subjection, but required with gentle sway,
> And by her yielded, by him best received.
>
> (4.297–309)

Their passage 'hand in hand' (4.321), besides constituting a naturalistic detail about human affection, no doubt carries a symbolic weight about their harmony and concord; but it is a concord between disparate entities. We see them, in a sense, through Satan's eyes; his conclusions are interpretations of the ethical significance of elements in their physical appearance. There is no suggestion, however, that he errs significantly. Indeed, as commentators remark, Milton's differentiation of the genders by means of their haircut is Pauline (I Corinthians 11:14–15 'Doth not even nature itself teach you, that, if a man have long hair, it is a shame unto him? But if a woman have long hair, it is a glory to her: for her hair is given her for a covering'). Paul's discourse, which unmistakeably shows through Milton's first account of Adam

and Eve, relates the matter of hair to the issue of power. It marks
the relationship between men and women, and the relationship
of both to the Godhead:

> For a man indeed ought not to cover his head, forasmuch as he is
> the image and glory of God: but the woman is the glory of the
> man. For the man is not of the woman; but the woman of the
> man. Neither was the man created for the woman; but the woman
> for the man.
>
> (11:7-9)

It could scarcely be clearer. Perhaps the clarity of Milton (as
of Paul) constitutes the only terms in which his discussion of
the paradigmatic relationships between men and women can be
defended. Just as Milton's (version of) God (in Empson's view)
demystifies the horror (if such it be) at the heart of Christianity, so
Milton's Edenic marriage demystifies the power relations implied
in Christian orthodoxy and inscribed in the cultural, social and
legal structures of his own age. Unlike contemporary and earlier
love poets, Milton comes clean on the real nature of heterosexual
love in his own and earlier ages; the servant–lover and his mistress
are set aside, and we see the patriarchal husband and his spouse.
Of course, Milton still speaks deeply and quite movingly of the
possibilities for real solace between the sexes, but his vision is
unclouded with poetic fancies. The inequality communicates
itself even in the nature of their sins. Eve sees her sin as a
double crime, both against God and against Adam: 'both [of
us] have sinned, but thou/Against God only, I against God and
thee' (10.930–1).

> Let your women keep silence in the churches: for it is not
> permitted unto them to speak; but they are commanded to be under
> obedience, as also saith the law. And if they will learn any thing, let
> them ask their husbands at home: for it is a shame for women to
> speak in the church.
>
> (I Corinthians 14:34–5)

Thus the apostle Paul, and Milton's epic nothing extenuates the
disabling sexism of Christian orthodoxy. But, as we shall see,
though he attributes to Adam all the responsibilities and privileges
of patriarchal authority, he nevertheless depicts Eve as characterised
by rationality and both courage and intellectual integrity, thus

extending to some extent the role left open to women by the sternest view of his contemporaries.

More than any other epic poem – and perhaps more than any other sustained narrative of major literary significance – *Paradise Lost* operates at a high level of philosophical intensity and complexity. In Books 9 and 10 many of the ethical problems central to the poem (and, Milton believed, central to human experience) enter a critical phase and achieve resolution. While Book 3, with its grand heavenly exposition of God's policy towards both people and angels, contains the central account of Milton's view of the Godhead and the larger course of world history, Books 9 and 10 work on a more intimate level to explore responsibilities, anxieties and challenges on a human scale.

Adam and Eve are confronted with a series of difficult decisions. Some they get right, others they get catastrophically wrong, but the first choice they make – to separate – is perhaps less grave than it is often represented to be, and the quality of their decision is much less certain.

The question is, should Adam and Eve split up to do their work, or should they stick together? With hindsight the reader (like Adam himself, 9.1134–8) perhaps thinks they should have opted for the latter course. But we should recall how carefully God has prepared the test which they are to undergo. He has permitted Satan to leave hell (1.212), he has watched his progress without intervening to hinder it (3.69–79), and he has in effect restrained the angelic guards which he had placed in Eden so they neither arrest nor assault Satan when they find him (4.1010–15). Moreover, to regulate the test and make it fair, he has supplied Adam and Eve with enough information for them to have some concept of how evil may be perpetrated (Books 5 and 6 contain the angel Raphael's description of Satan's frauds in the war in heaven); but he has not given them so much information as to forestall Satan's challenge – Raphael gave them no account of the nature of death. The test is desired, allowed, controlled and observed by God: had Adam and Eve that day stayed together to confront and perhaps confound Satan, there is no reason to suppose that a proper individual challenge would not be permitted or contrived at some later date. We should recall that Adam very specifically has been advised by Raphael that the long prospect of human history among those descended from him may well contain episodes of conflict in which some participants at least will be 'malicious' and therefore, he and we may assume, fallen. As Raphael describes the use of artillery in the war in heaven and relates it to human experience, he refers, not to what Adam experientially knows, but to what he is invited to contemplate as happening in the human future:

> yet haply of thy race
> In future days, if malice should abound,
> Some one intent on mischief, or inspired
> With devilish machination might devise
> Like instrument to plague the sons of men
> For sin, on war and mutual slaughter bent.

> (6.501–06)

Raphael isn't saying that humankind will fall; merely that 'haply', that is, 'maybe' or 'perchance', there may be some fallen people who behave as the fallen angels behave. But certainly Adam has every reason to think that eventually some of his descendants may choose wrongly and join the enemy.

Eve, substantially, is right in her claim that they have the potential to work better when separated; and she is right that their task, pleasant, constructive and welcome, is not only to populate the world but also to produce from creation's plenty a social and economic structure to support that population (9.205–25). Michael describes how such a society may have evolved, had they not fallen:

> this had been
> Perhaps thy capital seat, from when had spread
> All generations, and had hither come
> From all the ends of the earth, to celebrate
> And reverence thee their great progenitor.

> (11.342–6)

Eve is also right that she is of herself sufficiently well equipped to withstand the test which Satan's approach constitutes. Though Adam is anxious about her leaving, his last words stress that she remains in control of all the resources she needs to stand right until her voluntary capitulation to Satan's temptation: 'God towards

thee hath done his part, do thine' (9.375). The Father's point in
Book 3 had been that virtue, untempted, is unmeritorious; Eve
reiterates this notion in debate with Adam: 'And what is faith,
love, virtue unassayed/Alone . . . ?' (335–6). She makes the point
in terms analogous to those Milton himself adopted in *Areopagitica*
(1644), where he argues that a free press tests the virtuous by
exposing them to contrary opinion, as has often been remarked.

The second major matter of choice, Eve's decision to eat the
fruit, is immediately felt to be terribly wrong. The reader knows
this, as he or she has known it since his or her earliest and most
rudimentary religious instruction. The narrator tells us it is wrong,
and he shows us the response of 'Nature': 'Earth felt the wound,
and nature from her seat/Sighing through all her works gave signs
of woe' (9.782–3) (see below, Chapter 4). The question for the reader
is not whether Eve was right, but how could she, a perfect human
being, have been so tragically wrong.

Milton's answer rests in the complexity of the temptation he
depicts Satan creating for her. Adam has already shown himself
a shrewd observer of the operations of the human mind (for
example, in his comments on the origins of unpleasant dreams
– 5.95–121), and he has warned her of the limitations of reason:
'reason not impossibly may meet/Some specious object' (9.360–1).
God's interdiction of the fruit of one tree has a logic-defying
arbitrariness. Satan (and Eve as she falls) can make no sense of
it – why that tree? No reason. God needs give no reason, nor
could do: what is significant is the interdiction itself, not the
interdicted object. Indeed, when the covert Satan hears Adam
and Eve discuss the interdiction, he responds in a paroxysm of
bewilderment, delight and outrage:

> One fatal tree there stands of knowledge called,
> Forbidden them to taste: knowledge forbidden?
> Suspicious, reasonless. Why should their Lord
> Envy them that? Can it be sin to know,
> Can it be death? And do they only stand
> By ignorance, is that their happy state,
> The proof of their obedience and their faith?
> O fair foundation laid whereon to build
> Their ruin!

> (4.514–22)

Satan would find such an interdiction intolerable. 'Reasonless'! –

there is no *reason* why Adam and Eve should obey beyond God's utterly arbitrary dictat. The requirement to obey a reasonless rule makes a sterner test than the requirement to obey a rule which makes sense.

Eve engages the issue that the serpent puts to her quite logically, albeit that she works from the false premise that the serpent has eaten the fruit and, far from dying, has been improved by it. The conclusion that her reasoning leads her to accords well enough with the other assumptions she holds. Raphael had advised Adam and Eve that God intends some upward revision of their place in the scale of being, bringing them closer to angels (7.158–61). The promptings of Eve's reason are sharply juxtaposed with God's reasonless interdiction. The choice for a self-respecting person is disturbing – either obey against your reason or follow your reason and disobey, though, of course, Eve chooses incorrectly when she takes the latter option.

Her disastrous decision has about it certain elements of moral courage; if it is ill-informed, especially about the nature of death, that is because God has ensured the inadequacy of her information. Adam, too, acts in a way which, on the human scale, is courageous, even heroic, though his choice, like Eve's, reflects a very shallow understanding of death's nature and consequences. If they had been given the vision of horror, of murder, persecution and disease, which Michael shows Adam in Books 11 and 12 after they have fallen, either could well have evaluated the options rather differently. Dying a martyr to reason or to love has an attraction which palls when the fuller implications are appreciated.

Eve persuaded herself that she probably would not be punished for following reason: Adam knows very clearly that God will punish him for following Eve. The process of his fall contrasts sharply with Eve's. She has reasoned her way into trouble, whereas Adam, paradoxically, falls by not reasoning at all. Of course, obeying the interdiction against the forbidden fruit really needed no thinking about, but the heirs to Adam's misconduct may well feel that disobeying it merited a pause for reflection. Not so Adam; without consideration he announces 'Certain my resolution is to die' (9.907).

Readers have often wondered about the alternative courses of action which Adam could have taken. 'What should he have done?' is the question Milton insistently challenges us with. To a romantically inclined reader (especially, perhaps, one with a taste for grand opera) Adam's solution is, at least initially, appealing. Of course, the hero must die with his beloved. To think otherwise would be rather like rewriting *Romeo and Juliet* so that Juliet, waking to appreciate Romeo's tragic error, lives on, perhaps to marry someone more acceptable to her parents. Yet there were alternatives open to Adam. The opening lines of Book 9 allude to conversations with 'God or angel guest' (9.1). Formerly, Adam had discoursed with the Son and with angels: he is still sinless, he needs not fear them, and he has never so keenly required their counsel. He could urgently have sought their advice.

'Flesh of my flesh,/Bone of my bone', Adam intones (9.914–15). Milton, however, regarded the wedlock bond rather differently. Almost 25 years before the first publication of *Paradise Lost*, he had achieved some notoriety among fellow puritans for his advocacy of a relaxation of the law to permit divorce for reasons of incompatibility and to allow divorcees to remarry. Milton believed his proposed reforms came closest to remodelling the marriage bond into what God had originally intended, so we may assume that he regarded suing for divorce as at least an option open to Adam.

Such a policy, however, has a charmlessness about it. Though, as we shall see, Milton throughout *Paradise Lost* is redefining the notion of heroism (see below, Chapter 5), perhaps an Adam who petitions for divorce falls too far below readers' expectations, even if he were to make decent provision for Eve in her old age. What then should he have done? What was the *best* option, best both ethically and aesthetically? Danielson has recently advanced a cogent suggestion: Adam should have done what Christ does, die (or at least offer to die) *in place of* the sinner.[4]

Christian theology had for long regarded Adam as in some sense the imperfect forerunner of Christ. The connection is very ancient. Paul had written in 1 Corinthians 15:

21 For since by man came death, by man came also the resurrection of the dead.
22 For as in Adam all die, even so in Christ shall all be made alive.

45 And so it is written, The first man Adam was made a living soul; the last Adam was made a quickening spirit.

To relate the first Adam to Christ, the second Adam, was a commonplace of Biblical interpretation among Milton's contemporaries. In Book 3, Milton has already shown his readers Christ's response to a problem very similar to the one Adam faces. The Father assured the Son and the heavenly host that Adam and Eve will sin and would die forever unless someone volunteered to die in their place, and the Son had responded by undertaking to accept their punishment (3.227–302).

Why doesn't Adam arrive at this course of conduct? We should not too readily fault his courage. After he has fallen, in the depths of their despair, Eve suggests that she should ask God to punish her in his place, and he replies that he had already thought of offering to die himself and rejected it as unlikely to work (10.947–57). Anyway, by then the opportunity had passed.

SALVATION

No theological issue discussed in *Paradise Lost* receives as much explicit attention as the doctrine of salvation; on no matter of religious controversy is the doctrinal position of the poem so clearly established. Nor should this surprise us, for the debate to which Milton's poem contributes profoundly fissured the topography of English Christianity from the Reformation to the end of the seventeenth century.

How may postlapsarian humankind be saved? From Luther onward the Protestants responded firmly 'By faith alone'; this was in sharp conflict with the Roman Catholic position, which held that salvation could be effected through the agencies of good works or the intercession of third parties such as saints. The Lutheran position interiorises the most important issue facing the Christian believer. It removes salvation from the overview of institutionalised religion, which may no longer exact deeds or payments or courses of devotional exercises from those who would be saved. Moreover, it removes salvation from the realm of what is visible; it is a matter between the soul of the individual and the Godhead, no longer capable of external monitoring.

Calvin and his followers made clearer those doctrinal implications of salvation by faith alone which had remained largely implicit in Lutheran theology. The decision of the individual to behave in some sense meritoriously is set aside as irrelevant to personal salvation (good works are done by the godly, but no one is godly because he or she does good works), and notions of personal choice and personal decision in the scheme of salvation are displaced by the intervention of the Godhead through the agency of grace acting on the chosen individual. Choice – election – is transposed from the individual to the Godhead. One cannot choose whether one will receive grace and thus salvation. Indeed, none of us deserves it; all, strictly, deserve to be damned in that all share the inherited guilt of Adam and Eve's original sin. But out of mercy, not out of justice, God chooses some, the elect, that not all of his creation may be lost to Satan. Since God foreknows everything, he has foreknown, even before the creation of the world, those who are to be saved, and (in the grimmest version of this doctrine, what is termed 'double predestination') those who are to be damned.

Just as the doctrine of salvation by faith alone in the sixteenth century fissured Protestantism from Catholicism, so in the seventeenth century Protestantism itself was divided over the question of predestination. The issue became a heated one, first in the Dutch reformed church, then, particularly from about 1620 onwards, within the Church of England.[5] Arminius, a Dutch reformed divine of considerable eminence and influence, argued, contrary to Calvin's position, that the individual in some sense participated in his or her own salvation.

Arminianism, as the movement became known, argued that salvation originated in a synergy or collaboration between grace and the free will of the individual. It is premissed on the belief that, though all aspects of the human personality are corrupted by the effect of original sin, the Godhead (again as a work of mercy, rather than a work of justice) returns to all, in limited fashion, the capacity to use one's free will to choose to follow the right course towards salvation when it is presented by the effect of grace. Extreme Calvinism had divided all humankind into two fixed and predestined groups, the elect who are saved and the reprobate who are not, and may not, be saved. Arminianism, while it may accept that some are specially exempt from the process and chosen for special salvation, postulates that the ordinary run of humankind has the capacity to be saved if the individual will choose to cooperate with the action of grace. But merely choosing to be saved is not of itself an option. As Arminius puts it,

> In this [fallen] state, the free will of man towards the true good is
> not only wounded, maimed, infirm, bent, and weakened; but it is
> also imprisoned, destroyed, and lost. And its powers are not only
> debilitated and useless unless they be assisted by grace, but it has
> no powers whatsoever except such as are excited by divine grace.
> For Christ has said, 'Without me ye can do nothing'.[6]

The effect of the Lutheran and Calvinist reformations was, para-
doxically, to place the issue of salvation within the individual
consciousness and then to nullify the role of the individual in
participating in the process. Arminianism, in several ways, is a
psychologically liberating theology, repositioning the decision-
making on the human scale and contextualising it in personal
struggle rather than purely divine determination.

Arminianism in the English context assumed two rather different
manifestations which diverged in their larger ideological impli-
cations while retaining some common ground in theological the-
ory. What may be termed the episcopalian version was central to
the vision of that most influential of Caroline churchmen, William
Laud, Bishop of London from 1628, Archbishop of Canterbury
from 1633 till his execution in 1645, and by far the most powerful
divine of his age. Laud sought to revitalise the Church of England
and to reposition it within the hierarchy of political and cultural
institutions of the age. His programme addressed many aspects of
its perceived decline, from the wealth of its endowments and the
physical condition of its buildings to the order of its services. His
concern with 'the beauty of holiness' manifested itself in reforms
in church discipline and church finance and a reassertion of the role
of the clergy in the spiritual lives of the communities they served.
He was also an Arminian. Laudian Arminianism in effect revalued
the role of the clergy in the salvation of their congregations. Their
ministry was to function as a sort of catalyst in the reaction between
the free will of the believer and the grace extended to him or to
her. A commitment to the Arminian schema of salvation in some
sense constituted a Laudian innovation in the spiritual life of the
Church of England, and it separated Laud and his closest and
most trusted associates both from the earlier straightforwardly
Calvinist tradition in the church and from many contemporary
episcopalian Anglicans. However, his closeness to Charles I and
the King's personal support for his programme of reform ensured
that by the late 1630s Arminianism was a powerful and in some

ways dominant element within the church; certainly in the late 1630s in most dioceses no Anglican clergyman would have been jeopardising his career by subscribing to the Arminian view on the dogma of salvation.

But the mid-century saw the emergence of a radical Arminianism on the part of Milton and some others, principally, I believe, on the radical wing of independent congregationalism. For Milton, the external agency of the clergy has no relevance to the salvation of the individual believer. Radical Arminianism has all the interiority of the Lutheran and Calvinist positions, but it is reanimated by the active role of the believer in receiving and collaborating with grace. The congruence of this theological tenet with much else in mid-century radical thought is easy to surmise. This is a theology that liberates the individual to struggle alone for salvation outside the monolithic and unrelenting decree of the Godhead envisaged by Calvin and outside the meddling intervention, the spiritual brokerage, of the Anglican ministry.

However, the version of Arminianism to which Milton subscribed held, at the level of abstraction at which he works in *Paradise Lost*, absolutely no dangers for its subscribers in the Restoration period. In the 1650s, when we may assume Milton started work on his epic, radical Arminianism was a respected or at least tolerated position, though a minority one in a period dominated by Calvinistic versions of puritanical Protestantism; at the Restoration, while the doctrine never recaptured the pivotal significance it held in Anglican controversy in the 1630s, it became again in some ways the dominant position.

I began this section with an assertion that on no other theological issue is Milton so explicit. Besides being a topic that deeply exercised contemporary theologians, the doctrine of salvation was the one area of significant controversy in which Milton could be utterly open about his beliefs. About the relationship between the Father and the Son, if he were indeed (like the author of *Christian Doctrine*) heterodox, he would necessarily have to proceed with caution; so, too, on issues like the fate of the soul immediately after death (another point of heterodoxy in *Christian Doctrine*), about which *Paradise Lost* has something to say, but of a brief and relatively unclear nature (10.789–92; but see, too, 11.446–7). But on salvation his anti-Calvinism is both a controversial and a safe position.

He could scarcely be clearer. At the level of theory, Arminian salvation is expounded by the Father; and the level of practice, it is exemplified by the case histories of Adam and Eve.

Let us return to the theological core of the poem, the exchange between the Father and the Son in Book 3, and to the Father's speech, which we have in preliminary fashion considered above (Chapter 1):

> Man shall not quite be lost, but saved who will,
> Yet not of will in him, but grace in me
> Freely vouchsafed; once more I will renew
> His lapsed powers, though forfeit and enthralled
> By sin to foul exorbitant desires;
> Upheld by me, yet once more he shall stand
> On even ground against his mortal foe,
> By me upheld, that he may know how frail
> His fallen condition is, and to me owe
> All his deliverance, and to none but me.
> Some I have chosen of peculiar grace
> Elect above the rest; so is my will:
> The rest shall hear me call, and oft be warned
> Their sinful state, and to appease betimes
> The incensed Deity, while offered grace
> Invites; for I will clear their senses dark,
> What may suffice, and soften stony hearts
> To pray, repent, and bring obedience due.
> To prayer, repentance, and obedience due,
> Though but endeavoured with sincere intent,
> Mine ear shall not be slow, mine eye not shut.
> And I will place within them as a guide
> My umpire conscience, whom if they will hear,
> Light after light well used they shall attain,
> And to the end persisting, safe arrive.
> This my long sufferance and my day of grace
> They who neglect and scorn, shall never taste;
> But hard be hardened, blind be blinded more,
> That they may stumble on, and deeper fall;
> And none but such from mercy I exclude.

                                                        (3.173–202)

Note that the Father's exposition is essentially Ramist. First he divides those to whom 'peculiar grace' is extended from the rest; then he divides the rest into those who hear his call and respond and those who hear his call and ignore it. 'Peculiar' is a word of some currency in Calvinist discourse as an attribute of the elect. Norton's translation of Calvin's *Institutes* remarks that God reserves 'some peculiar thing concerning his electes'.[7] A contemporary angelologist vouchsafed the opinion that 'It is probably that every elect hath his proper and peculiar Angell'.[8] Milton, evidently, concedes at the outset that the Godhead, in its inexplicable mercy, extends a special or distinct grace to some who are 'Elect above the rest' and who are exempt from the struggles of the rest. 'So is my will' excludes this element in divine policy from the critique by human reason.

God notes this special group and then straight away sets them aside. The second group is dichotomised into those who hear and heed and those who hear and heed not. How they respond to the invitations of offered grace determines their fate. They are not saved because they choose to heed (they cannot will or effect their own salvations); but if they do not choose to heed then they are excluded from salvation. Milton describes salvation not as an instantaneous event but as a process in which the individual believer interacts with the prompting and the illumination of the spirit. Those on the salvation track pray and repent, but Milton stresses that these actions are not sufficient in themselves to secure salvation; rather, they secure salvation because the merciful Father, taking the intention for the achievement, deems these actions meritorious. He responds with further aid, 'light after light' and above all 'my umpire conscience'; an umpire, presumably, in that conscience lets the regenerate judge between the alternative courses which persistently confront them in the fallen world. Those who hear but do not heed receive the opposite treatment. Instead of light after light, the 'blind be blinded more' and their damnation, through their refusal to cooperate with the grace extended to the worst of sinners, is justified and confirmed.

In the history of Satan and his angels Milton shows us the process of moral degeneration in the case of those excluded from salvation, though of course the fallen angels are excluded by God's judgement, whereas fallen humans are excluded only if they decline to heed what they hear. The fates of the fallen angels constitute case histories in the Calvinist doctrine of reprobation; that doctrine, however, does not apply to humankind (see Chapter 2).[9] In the regeneration of Adam and Eve, Milton gives an extended spiritual case history of the process of regeneration as represented in Arminian doctrine.

That process is the matter of Adam's monologue and his dialogue with Eve extending from 10.720 to the end of that book. Adam begins with a series of exclamations and questions, alternating something akin to reproach for God's justice with recognitions of his own culpability and his sense of how badly he is reacting to the punishment which has been imposed on him: 'Did I request thee, Maker, from my clay/To mould me man . . . ?' (10.743–4); 'Inexplicable/ Thy justice seems; yet to say truth, too late,/I thus contest' (10.754–6); 'Ah, why should all mankind/For one man's fault thus guiltless be condemned,/If guiltless? But from me what can proceed,/But all corrupt . . . ?' (10.822–5). The outcome of this inner struggle is Adam's recognition and acknowledgement of his sinfulness; this sense of conviction, however, yields no immediate prospect of spiritual advancement in that Adam erroneously concludes that his case parallels Satan in its hopelessness:

> [Adam speaks:] Thus what thou [i.e., Adam]
>   desirest
> And what thou fear'st, alike destroys all hope
> Of refuge, and concludes thee miserable
> Beyond all past example and future,
> To Satan only like both crime and doom.
> O conscience! into what abyss of fears
> And horrors hast thou driven me; out of which
> I find no way, from deep to deeper plunged!
>
> (10.837–44)

In a sense Adam's suffering is accentuated by his ignorance: the only case of crime and punishment he knows is that of the fallen angels, and Michael's vision of the future will certainly allow him to differentiate between levels of culpability on the part of fallen humankind. His conscience, however painful, however 'evil' (10.849) in the sense of being a consciousness of his own evil doing, leads him to a first stage, in that he recognises that the counter arguments he transitionally entertained about God's unfairness cannot be sustained. Recognition of those truths which he needs in order to become regenerate emerge not in inner meditation but in debate, as so often in the Milton oeuvre. (Compare the experience of Samson and the case of Abdiel, discussed above, Chapter 2.)

Eve approaches:

> Whom thus afflicted when sad Eve beheld,
> Desolate where she sat, approaching nigh,
> Soft words to his fierce passion she assayed . . .
>
> (10.863–5)

Note the significance of the syntactical ambiguity: 'desolate' is a shared epithet; desolate Eve beholds Adam to be desolate. They sinned together; they suffer together; they regenerate together. Milton attributes enormous importance to the relationship in the revival they each experience; it constitutes his profoundest appreciation of the role of the companionate marriage of the godly in the fallen world.

Eve behaves utterly contritely towards Adam, in a fashion that renders his initial hostility, a tissue of misogynistic clichés, as Fowler observes (10.884–8n), immature and untenable: 'both have sinned, but thou/Against God only, I against God and thee' (10.930–1), she acknowledges. Adam makes the first regenerative step in forgiving her, and he does so in terms which define the role of godly matrimony in a hostile world:

> But rise, let us no more contend, nor blame
> Each other, blamed enough elsewhere, but strive
> In offices of love, how we may lighten
> Each other's burden in our share of woe . . .
>
> (10.958–61)

Following his finer instincts and prompted by a recollection of love, he has stumbled into acting on a central tenet of Christianity, forgiving her that trespassed against him; he, too, will be forgiven.

Eve, 'recovering heart' (10.966), responds to his action in terms which have a profound resonance within the poem. She speaks of herself as 'Restored by thee, vile as I am, to place/Of new acceptance, hopeful to regain/Thy love' (10.971–3). Restoration is the role of the Son. The whole poem opens within an anticipation of the time when 'one greater man/[shall] Restore us' (1.4–5). More explicitly, the Father tells the Son:

> be thou in Adam's room
> The head of all mankind, though Adam's son.
> As in him perish all men, so in thee
> As from a second root shall be restored,
> As many as are restored, without thee none
>
> (3.285–9)

Curiously and proleptically, Adam in forgiving Eve performs an *imitatio Christi* which restores her as the Son will restore all of humankind.

The solutions which Eve postulates to the problems now faced by their species, while meritoriously contemptuous of human happiness, do not, as Adam recognises, conform to the terms of the sentence passed on them by the Son; they cannot simply not breed or not live, because they are obliged to labour and to bear children. However, meeting her points calls for the engagement of Adam's rational faculties, linked to a pious resolve to accept the punishment designated for them. In place of her 'vehement despair' (10.1007), 'Adam . . . /To better hopes his more attentive mind/Labouring had raised' (10.1010–12). 'Labouring'! In the sweat of his brow Adam progresses to his (and her) salvation. But not by works. Rather, his inner struggle, led on by light after light, constitutes the synergy of will and grace. Nevertheless the individual's role is explicitly and unflinchingly an active one. A critical point in Adam's argument is passed when he tells Eve:

>   let us seek
> Some safer resolution, which methinks
> I have in view, calling to mind with heed
> Part of our sentence, that thy seed shall bruise
> The serpent's head . . .
>
>   (10.1028–32)

Thus he recognises that the sentence is also a promise; he does so through a sequence of mental feats. He calls to mind, he takes heed, and together they can seek.

They seek and they find. The book ends with recognition that the Son comes in mercy as well as judgement; in this light, they can repair to their place of judgement and in hope of further grace offer their prayers, 'sent from hearts contrite, in sign/Of sorrow unfeigned, and humiliation meek' (10.1103–4).

AFTER THE FALL

The critical commonplace that Books 11 and 12 constitute some sort of falling off, as if Milton the marathon–runner had hit some sort of intellectual glycogen depletion, has been displaced by some vigorous and intelligent readings which recognise their thematic and ideological sigificance within the poem.[10] Of course, we have no evidence that the final books were written last, while there is every reason to suppose that the whole has been assiduously revised.

What Milton demonstrates in the prophetic images and the narrative Michael vouchsafes to Adam is a version of postlapsarian history as a pattern of individual resistance to corrupt, sinful and violent societies. Within the poem the pattern is anticipated in Abdiel's solitary resistance within the Satanic legion, as '[t]he flaming seraph fearless, though alone/Encompassed round with foes' (5.875-6) answers his erstwhile leader in the language of the godly, for which he is eventually rewarded with divine approbation:

> Servant of God, well done, well hast thou fought
> The better fight, who single hast maintained
> Against revolted multitudes the cause
> Of truth, in word mightier than they in arms . . .

> (6.29-32)

But Milton, in the greatest of his late prose works, had already celebrated the role of the beleaguered godly in his representation of himself as a prophet steeled against the persecution he keenly anticipates:

> Thus much I should perhaps have said though I were sure I should have spoken only to trees and stones; and had none to cry to, but with the Prophet, *O earth, earth, earth!* to tell the very soil it self, what her perverse inhabitants are deaf to. (*Readie and Easie Way to Establish a Free Commonwealth*, second edition, *CPW*, 7, revised edition, 462-3)

Holstun, who has also connected these passages, sees Milton as configuring an image of himself as both prophet and martyr, indeed as a Christ figure who prophesies his own martyrdom. That pattern of associations is central to Milton's view of history (and of the role of the godly within it), though the late prose work simultaneously struggles to avert the catastrophe which its symbolic scheme anticipates.[11]

Though Milton's brief histories of the Hebrew people and the Christian church cannot be read as sustained *roman à clef* to the political events of his own age, his theory of human history, that it is a cycle of folly which will only be halted by the end of history at the second coming, necessarily invites equations between the events of his own age and earlier crises and disasters. What Adam is made to see is a process which, as a republican idealist, Milton may have thought had been halted in the commonwealth of the saints

ushered in by the execution of Charles I; but human perverseness
could not sustain the moral standards of that free commonwealth,
and the pattern of general depravity and individual heroism was
scarcely checked and, by 1667, was grotesquely flourishing (see
below, Chapter 6).

What of the scenes and episodes of the concluding books?
Some, of course, address primarily the physiological imperatives
of postlapsarian human experience, particularly the forms of death
and geriatric decay; the second vision, 11.475–99, in particular treats
these issues, and supports an ethical statement about the importance
of continence and moderation. The first vision, of Cain's murder
of Abel, stresses the earthly victory of the ungodly and the
postponement of the reward of the godly:

> the unjust the just hath slain,
> For envy that his brother's offering found
> From heaven acceptance; but the bloody fact
> Will be avenged, and the other's faith approved
> Lose no reward, though here thou see him die,
> Rolling in dust and gore.

(11.455–60)

Abel thus becomes the archetype for godly martyrs who have
'groaned out their souls' (a curious phrase for a mortalist) in
bloody tableaux of defeat in the marketplaces and execution sites
of the world, most memorably (by 1667) at Tyburn and Charing
Cross where, in the early years of the Restoration, regicides were
executed; the massive effusion of blood, foregrounded in Milton's
description, was often remarked on as a conspicuous element of
execution by hanging, drawing and quartering.

The third vision, of the tents of the descendants of Lamech,
supports another ethical thesis, about the role of godly marriage
in safeguarding personal integrity and about how court amours
subvert godliness. 'Judge not what is best/By pleasure', advises
Michael (11.603–04), and his analysis of the role of female licen-
tiousness in the corrosion of society at once comments on the
events of the vision and asserts transhistorical truths as applicable
to the Restoration court as to the scene from Hebrew history:

> For that fair female troop thou saw'st, that seemed
> Of goddesses, so blithe, so smooth, so gay,
> Yet empty of all good wherein consists

Woman's domestic honour and chief praise;
Bred only and completed to the taste
Of lustful appetance, to sing, to dance,
To dress, and troll the tongue and roll the eye.

(11.614–20)

The voice of the narrator has already warned against court amours
and their associated evils (4.765–70; see above); Michael stresses that,
seductive though the women are, the primary responsibility rests
in masculine control of both male and female appetite:

From man's effeminate slackness it begins,
Said the angel, who should better hold his place
By wisdom, and superior gifts received.

(11.634–6)

The masculinist agenda, clearly articulated in the context of the
paradisal relationship, carries at least as much importance in the
fallen world. The male saint must control himself and his spouse;
but their marriage bond fashions a vital mechanism in their
ideological survival; within the family and through mutual support
they may endure.[12]

The fourth vision depicts an experience closest to that of Abdiel
as Enoch bears prophetic witness against the corruptions of his own
society in a way that is simultaneously reminiscent of Milton's own
prophetic stance in the last days of the republic:

anon
Gray-headed men and grave, with warriors mixed,
Assemble, and harangues are heard, but soon
In factious opposition, till at last
Of middle age one rising, eminent
In wise deport, spake much of right and wrong,
Of justice, of religion, truth, and peace,
And judgment from above: him old and young
Exploded and had seized with violent hands,
Had not a cloud descending snatched him thence
Unseen amid the throng . . .

(11.661–71)

Again, I am reminded of the way Milton (aged 51) represented
himself in *The Readie and Easie Way*, a pamphlet twice issued amid
the harangues and wranglings of civilian *and military* republicans
which characterised the opening months of 1660 (and the end of

the republic). There he memorialised his own role as a champion
who had single-handedly defended the righteousness of the coup
of 1649 against 'superstition and tyranny' (*CPW*, 7, revised edition,
420–1), while asseverating that he, only he, still spoke the language
of the Good Old Cause, a language shared with the prophets of
the Old Testament.

As I have remarked elsewhere, a fear of the multitude stalks the
pages of his late republican pamphlets.[13] Certainly, the rewards of
his final efforts were ridicule and abuse, like the reward of Enoch.
Recall his comments. how he is:

> fallen on evil days,
> On evil days though fallen, and evil tongues;
> In darkness, and with dangers compassed round,
> And solitude.

(7.25–8)

However, Milton's experience differed sharply in that 'violent
hands' probably did seize him; no cloudy assumption for the
godly remnant of 1660.[14] Michael once more generalises about
the vision Adam has been confronted with:

> But he the seventh from thee, whom thou beheld'st
> The only righteous in a world perverse,
> And therefore hated. therefore so beset
> With foes for daring singly to be just,
> And utter odious truth, that God would come
> To judge them with his saints . . .

(11.700–05)

Ever thus, Michael implies; utter truth and this is the consequence,
and yet the godly must always bear witness to the truth, irre-
spective of consequences.

The fifth and final vision offers another version of the 'one
just man alive' (11.818), Noah this time, who escapes through
a special providence when God punishes alike the dominators
and the formerly godly who have compromised in their period
of political eclipse – as Fowler notes, several editors have seen
contemporary allusion here (11.797–806n) – 'One man except, the
only son of light/In a dark age' (11.808-9).

With the Flood the sequence of dumbshows ends and Michael
adopts a prophetic narrative mode to define subsequent recurrences
of social corruption and individual heroism. Folly follows folly,

and again the events are represented in ways that connect the archetypal corruptions to the corruptions of his own age. A long golden age of republican 'paternal rule' is shattered by the rise of kingship. Nimrod, '[o]f proud ambitious heart', will prove:

> not content
> With fair equality, fraternal state,
> Will arrogate dominion undeserved
> Over his brethren, and quite dispossess
> Concord and law of nature from the earth . . .
>
> (12.25–9)

This indeed is 'empire tyrannous' (32) for explicitly it is the supremacy of an individual over his equals; Nimrod is no Tutbury stallion (see above, Chapter 2). Milton makes a great deal of this brief episode (verses in Genesis 10 and 11), no doubt because he wishes Adam to articulate clearly that kingship is of postlapsarian, not paradisal, origin, and thus Adam concludes:

> O execrable son so to aspire
> Above his brethren, to himself assuming
> Authority usurped, from God not given:
> He gave us only over beast, fish, fowl
> Dominion absolute; that right we hold
> By his donation; but man over men
> He made not lord; such title to himself
> Reserving, human left from human free
>
> (12.64–71)

Under the difficult circumstances in which Milton lived and wrote he could scarcely be clearer. Those royalist apologists who would have us regard Adam as the archetypal king and a justification for monarchy have from his own mouth the rehearsal of the counter argument. Adam knows what God told him, what he placed within his dominion, and it did not include other men (though, one might observe, it evidently did include women).

The further tribulations which Milton selects from the course of Hebrew history define once more the pattern of societal decay and individual heroism. Moral turpitude brings political subjugation and the crime of idolatry; Abraham and Moses are differentiated from the mass of corruption; 'the rest/Were long to tell' (12.260–1). Indeed so, but the narrative rushes now to its pivotal phase, the prophecy of the incarnation and the atonement.

When it comes, it accords closely with the recurrent pattern of human history. Christ, too, is the one just man of his age, and his life and death fit the scheme:

> he shall live hated, be blasphemed,
> Seized on by force, judged, and to death condemned
> A shameful and accurst, nailed to the cross
> By his own nation, slain for bringing life . . .

(12.411–14)

The incarnate Son embodies in its definitive form the solitary spiritual hero viciously assaulted by the unjust society ('his own nation') that he confronts with its own unrighteousness. After his death the pattern continues, except that now the godly are fortified by the Holy Spirit within them.

Once more, though chronologically Michael would seem to speak of an early era – here the apostolic period – his account defines species of depravity and folly current in Milton's own age:

> on earth
> Who against faith and conscience can be heard
> Infallible? Yet many will presume:
> Whence heavy persecution shall arise
> On all who in the worship persevere
> Of spirit and truth; the rest, far greater part,
> Well deem in outward rites and specious forms
> Religion satisfied; truth shall retire
> Bestuck with slanderous darts, and works of faith
> Rarely be found: so shall the world go on,
> To good malignant, to bad men benign . . .

(12.528–38)

The issues of the role of the civil magistrate in matters of conscience profoundly concerned Milton, and had been the subject of a pamphlet, written in 1659 in the Indian summer of the republic, entitled *A Treatise of Civil power in Ecclesiastical causes: shewing That it is not lawfull for any power on earth to compell in matters of Religion.* The workings of the spiritual life fall within the realm of Christ's governance, not that of the civil magistrate:

> Christ hath a government of his own, sufficient of it self to all his ends and purposes in governing his church; but much different from that of the civil magistrate; and the difference in this verie thing principally

consists, that it governs not by outward force . . . it deals only with
the inward man and his action, which are all spiritual . . .

(CPW, 7, revised edition, 255)

1659 was a year of republican optimism, at least into the high
summer when the tract was published; by 1667, truth, explicitly,
has retired. Between the prose and poetry comes a process of
withdrawal, of retreat into a defensive interiority. But the epic
speaks, too, of those clergy who not only take civil power but
also take 'names,/Places and titles' (12.515–16); the spirit of the old
antiprelatical campaigner – and of the anti-Presbyterian who had
excoriated the ambitions of some puritan clergy in the mid-1640s
– is clearly to be discerned (see Chapter 6).

> So shall the world go on . . . till the day
> Appear of respiration to the just,
> And vengeance to the wicked, at return
> Of him so lately promised to thy aid.

(12.537, 539–42)

Michael ties his account of what happens after the Ascension
of Christ to what happens throughout Milton's own age, and
throughout all ages till that final 'respiration', that second coming
with which all history ends. Till then, the godly have much to
endure.

NOTES

1. See Anna K. Nardo, 'Academic Interludes in *Paradise Lost*', *Milton Studies*, 27 (1991), pp. 209–41.

2. Lovelace, p. 76.

3. For the fullest account of contemporary views of pre- and postlapsarian sexuality, see James Grantham Turner, *One Flesh: Paradisal Marriage and Sexual Relations in the Age of Milton* (Oxford: Clarendon Press, 1987).

4. Dennis Danielson, 'Through the Telescope of Typology: What Adam Should Have Done', *Milton Quarterly*, 23 (1989), pp. 121–7.

5. Nicholas Tyacke, *The Rise of English Arminianism, c. 1590–1640* (Oxford: Clarendon, 1987).

6. Quoted by Carl Bangs, *Arminius: A Study in the Dutch Reformation* (Nashville and New York: Abingdon, 1971), p. 341.

7. Norton (1561), 2.82.

8.   Henry Lawrence, *Of our Communion and Warre with Angels* (London, 1646), p. 20.

9.   Stachniewski, especially Chapter 8.

10. See, especially, David Loewenstein, *Milton and the Drama of History: Historical Vision, Iconoclasm, and the Literary Imagination* (Cambridge: Cambridge University Press, 1990), especially Chapter 5.

11. James Holstun, *A Rational Millennium: Puritan Utopias of Seventeenth-Century England and America* (New York and Oxford: Oxford University Press, 1987), pp. 262–3; Corns, *Uncloistered Virtue*, pp. 290–2.

12. Keeble, especially Chapters 2 and 7.

13. Corns, *Uncloistered Virtue*, p. 290.

14. On Milton's incarceration in the final months of 1660, see William Riley Parker, *Milton: A Biography* (Oxford: Clarendon Press, 1968), Vol 1 pp. 575–76; on the ridicule he received, see J. Milton French, *The Life Records of John Milton* (1949–58; New York: Gordian, 1968), Vol 4, pp. 321, 326, 332–4, 337, 352–3.

Chapter 4

Chaos and the Created World

Mankind knows how the world was created through the revelation of the holy ghost to the putative author of Genesis, Moses. There is another source of information available in *Paradise Lost*, the knowledge given to Adam (and Eve) through the agency of Raphael, appointed to the task by the Father. Adam's first inkling about how the world he inhabits came into being comes in Raphael's prefatory remarks to his account of the war in heaven (see above, Chapter 2); it starkly juxtaposes chaos and creation: 'As yet this world was not, and Chaos wild/Reigned where these heavens now roll, where earth now rests' (5.577–8). After the account of the war, recollection of this becomes Adam's starting point for asking after the details of creation:

> what cause
> Moved the creator in his holy rest
> Through all eternity so late to build
> In chaos.
>
> (7.90–3)

As Raphael's account makes clear, the universe mankind inhabits is not only made in chaos but it is also made out of chaos.

Two alternative views were available to Milton in the Christian tradition. God could be deemed to have created the universe out of nothing or else out of matter the existence of which necessarily antedated the creation. The account in *Paradise Lost* plainly and unequivocally subscribes to the latter position. The Son, accompanied with a stately but curious 'procession' of good angels, rides '[f]ar into chaos, and the world unborn' (presumably the site where the world is to be born) and there the universe is marked off by 'the golden compasses' which he turns round 'through the vast profundity obscure', thus demarcating the matter to be transformed from the matter that is to remain as chaos at least for the time being (7.218–30).

Chaos is neither sufficient for the process of creation nor in itself wholly good for that purpose. It contains 'black tartareous cold infernal dregs/Adverse to life' which must be 'downward purged' before the universe can come into being (7.237–9). 'Tartareous', 'of or pertaining to Tartarus', a word Milton twice uses as a simple synonym for hell (2.858, 6.54); some constituent elements of chaos are good only for building the infernal prison house, and indeed that hell explicitly (the Father is speaking) has some of the characteristics of chaos:

> their place of punishment, the gulf
> Of Tartarus, which ready opens wide
> His fiery chaos to receive their fall.
>
> (6.53–5)

Hell, like the universe, is an encroachment on chaos, a displacement of chaos by something ordered and purposeful, as the personified figure of Chaos tells Satan as he crosses his territory en route from hell to earth (2.1002–06).

Just as chaos contains infernal dregs which must be expelled (and the Godhead palpably has a purpose for such matter), so too it lacks the life principle which animates the universe, and it lacks light. The raw material which constitutes it is made up of the four elements, earth, air, fire and water; it contains no light. The realm of 'Chaos' is also the realm of 'ancient' or 'eternal Night', the condition which obtains before the infusion of light. Light, literally, is a 'quintessence', a fifth element not found in the riot of atomic primaries in chaos but brought to it by the first command:

> Let there be light, said God, and forthwith light
> Ethereal, first of things, quintessence pure
> Sprung from the deep, and from her native east
> To journey through the airy gloom began, .
> Sphered in a radiant cloud, for yet the sun
> Was not; she in a cloudy tabernacle
> Sojourned the while. God saw the light was good . . .
>
> (7.243–9)

That seemingly perfunctory epithet 'first of things' draws attention by its incongruity amid such grandiloquence. Light is a 'thing', a physical entity, not merely a property or an effect. The Genesis

account, which has the creation of light precede the creation of
the sun and the moon (1:3, 14–18), had posed problems throughout
the commentary tradition: for Milton, it accords well with his
notion of the properties of light. Its arrival, albeit in a potential
or designate role, signals the marking off of the created universe
from the remaining realm of Chaos and Night. When the sun is
formed, light fills it as a liquid may fill a sponge:

> Of light by far the greater part he took,
> Transplanted from her cloudy shrine, and placed
> In the sun's orb, made porous to receive
> And drink the liquid light, firm to retain
> Her gathered beams, great palace now of light.
>
> (7.359–63)

The other bodies in some sense 'borrow' their light from the sun, the
moon by reflection, the stars and planets by reflection or 'tincture'
(7.367), an alchemical term implying a dilution of that primary element.

Note that Milton speaks of 'light ethereal', which prompts
recollection of an earlier account of the heavenly characteristics
of light in the invocation to Book 3 which precedes his direct
representation of the Godhead in heaven:

> Hail, holy Light, offspring of heaven first-born,
> Or of the eternal co-eternal beam
> May I express thee unblamed? since God is light,
> And never but in unapproached light
> Dwelt from eternity, dwelt then in thee,
> Bright effluence of bright essence increate.
> Or hear'st thou rather pure ethereal stream,
> Whose fountain who shall tell? Before the sun,
> Before the heavens thou wert, and at the voice
> Of God, as with a mantle didst invest
> The rising world of waters dark and deep,
> Won from the void and formless infinite.
>
> (3.1–12)

The tentativeness of Milton's exposition, which sits curiously
within this declarative, apostrophic mode, encapsulates the sense
that here he is up against the limits of human understanding of
the limitlessness of the divine. 'God *is* light' (the phrase is Biblical,
directly from 1 John 1:5), but how may we understand that vexing
copula? God 'dwells' in light (on the authority of 1 Timothy 6:16).

Does he both dwell in it and, in some sense, consist of it? Do we approach in pure light the essence of the Godhead? In the context of the created world the Godhead invokes light, so could he both be it and create it? Whatever is the case, it is to be worshipped and celebrated, though it cannot be fully comprehended by humans or indeed by any creature. Whether it is a product ('off-spring') or a constituent of the Godhead, 'co-eternal' with that eternal beam, may not be known. Where it comes from, its origin, its 'fountain', 'Who shall tell?' Even the notion that the issue (probably) passes understanding is couched in the interrogative mood.

'Ethereal', as Milton uses it, is a complex word. Sometimes, seemingly, it means no more than relating to the heavens. Thus, Satan's shield is termed 'ethereal temper' (1.285), presumably tempered in the ethereal or heavenly realms. But 'ether' meant, too, in effect, the quintessence, the purer substance from which purer beings and entities were fashioned (*OED*, 'ethereal' 2; 'ether' 2). Thus, the sun is 'of ethereal mould' (7.356); the fact that Milton says it was nevertheless 'unlightsome first' (7.355) suggests the usual interconnectedness of light and ether. I think there is reason to suppose Milton offers light and ether as two forms of a single essence. Its materiality in either manifestation, however, seems plainly asserted; the material of heaven is of 'ethereal mould' (2.139); angels' bodies are of 'ethereal substance' (6.330), and Milton's commitment to their materiality has already been demonstrated (see above, Chapter 2).

In his fuller account of the creation Milton is significantly vague about the origins of light. God does not simply command it to be (which would run counter to his concerns with representing the creation as a transmutation of extant matter). It '[s]prung from the deep' (7.245); it journeys (and the trip takes time) 'from her native east/To journey through the airy gloom' (7.245–6). 'Her' (rather than 'his', Milton's usual neuter genitive pronoun) personifies 'light'; it does not make the concept any easier to understand. 'The deep' is a mystery, an infinitude beyond the capacity of human (or probably angelic) comprehension, lying beneath and beyond and around what is known or imaginable. The fallen angels consider they may have to do God's 'errands' in 'the gloomy deep' (1.152); it is 'vast and boundless' (1.177); it is adjacent to hell and lies also between hell and heaven (2.79, 131, 7.134, 10.245); sometimes, it seems, it is synonymous with chaos (7.216) or hell or else its location (6.716); chaos is 'spread . . . on the wasteful deep' (2.960–1) or else is located within 'the hoary deep, a dark/Illimitable ocean without bound' (2.891-2). 'The deep' is and is to remain a problem and a mystery; indeed, it figures among the list of issues Michael advises Adam it would not profit him to know about in the fallen world, along with the names and characters of angels and the names of the stars (12.578). It functions, in its repetition throughout the poem, as the token of the great uncertainties which surround even the largest human understanding of the universe we inhabit.

The representation of chaos is always negative and frightening in *Paradise Lost*, though Milton is philosophically committed to regarding it a primary matter awaiting further divine intervention and organisation.[1] How may those issues be reconciled? Milton invests much in the description of chaos. He personifies it, paradoxically, as the ruler of anarchy; he neologises the substantive 'anarch' (2.988) to define such a reign, with the added contradiction that 'Chaos' rules over 'chaos'. Its central characteristics are best described when Satan journeys through it from hell to earth at the end of Book 2:

> eldest Night
> And Chaos, ancestors of Nature, hold
> Eternal anarchy, amidst the noise
> Of endless wars, and by confusion stand.
> For Hot, Cold, Moist, and Dry, four champions fierce
> Strive here for mastery, and to battle bring
> Their embryon atoms; they around the flag
> Of each his faction, in their several clans,
> Light-armed or heavy, sharp, smooth, swift or slow,
> Swarm populous, unnumbered as the sands
> Of Barca or Cyrene's torrid soil,
> Levied to side with warring winds, and poise
> Their lighter wings. To whom these most adhere,
> He rules a moment; Chaos umpire sits,
> And by decision more embroils the fray
> By which he reigns: next him high arbiter
> Chance governs all . . .
>   all these . . . thus must ever fight,
> Unless the almighty maker them ordain
> His dark materials to create more worlds . . .

(2.894–916)

What we have is the raw material left over after the construction of our world, available for the 'maker''s transmutation. That action gives order and providential purpose to inchoate matter which otherwise combines only randomly. Indeed, randomness, 'Chance', is the central informing (and deforming) principle of chaos, except that, beside the aleatory principle, a second chaotic principle works to ensure that such randomness, unlike the monkey and the typewriter, never serendipitously produces anything. Serendipity is expressly excluded.

That is why chaos, though philosophically neutral, appears so awful to the human consciousness. It sets at nothing the notions of providence and divine purpose. Until God determines on its transformation or until he suspends their operation, the two principles of chaos are allowed untrammelled performance. Thus, when Satan crosses chaos en route to earth, the success of his journey is determined by the characteristics of the medium through which he travels:

> all unawares
> Fluttering his pennons vain plumb down he drops
> Ten thousand fathom deep, and to this hour
> Down had been falling, had not by ill chance
> The strong rebuff of some tumultuous cloud
> Instinct with fire and nitre hurried him
> As many miles aloft . . .
>
> (2.932–8)

God chooses not to intervene providentially in the action of those physical rules. One chance takes Satan in a deep dive utterly beyond his control; another chance blows him upwards and, randomly, facilitates his approach to our world. Curiously, though, after the Fall, Sin and Death are allowed, in a clumsy parody of divine ordering of primal matter, to construct a causeway from earth to hell, '[h]overing upon the waters' to make a crude structure held together by 'asphaltic slime' (10.282–305). Moreover, just as chaos constitutes the condition of matter before creation, it may well constitute the condition into which the created world will be resolved at the end of its time: it is '[t]he womb of nature and perhaps her grave' (2.911).

NATURE AND FECUNDITY

That systems be allowed to operate according to their inherent characteristics is central to Milton's view of the creation, and the notion functions, too, to obviate a problem some had discerned in trying to make sense of the Genesis account, namely, why

God should have needed six days to perform the task if he is, by definition, omnipotent.[2] The account of his labours and his needs for rest smack of physical limitations on his transcendence. Raphael notes, 'Immediate are the acts of God' (7.176), but they can only be understood by humans if they are related to time and space. The Father dismisses the notion of physical limitation quite explicitly as he announces his policy for a new world:

> But lest [Satan's] heart exalt him in the harm
> Already done, to have dispeopled heaven
> My damage fondly deemed, I can repair
> That detriment, if such it be to lose
> Self-lost, and in a moment will create
> Another world, out of one man a race
> Of men innumerable, there to dwell . . .
>
> (7.150–6)

He goes on to say that, eventually, the human race will inhabit heaven. He could simply make new inhabitants for heaven, but he chooses not to. Instead, he establishes the process by which, 'out of one man' (and one woman), an innumerable population will be generated, and he sets in train the process of world history, stretching from 4004 BC, or thereabouts, to the millennium. Process is the key.

Milton's version of creation is a celebration of earth's systemic fertility:

> on the watery calm
> His brooding wings the spirit of God outspread,
> And vital virtue infused, and vital warmth
> Throughout the fluid mass.
>
> (7.234–7)

'Brood' is usually a female role; the word literally applies to incubating eggs. But the gendering ('his . . . wings'), and the vocabulary suggests something of the male sexual act, as the covering transfers 'virtue' and 'warmth' to the passive, recipient form which is thereby rendered fertile. The gendering of the earth is equally clear ('earth self balanced on her centre hung' – 7.242). Note that this additional element must be infused into the matter defined from chaos before the reproductivity of the universe is initiated. After the earth is formed it is 'in the womb as yet/Of waters, embryon immature' (7.276–7).

Several of the other phases of creation find representation in similar terms. That 'embryon' earth becomes 'the great mother' which conceives and brings forth hills and mountains (7.281–90). The phrase in Genesis, 'Let the waters bring forth abundantly' (1:20), already heavy with implications of fertility, finds further emphasis in Milton as the waters 'generate/Reptile with spawn abundant' (7.387–8), so that creeks and bays '[w]ith fry innumerable swarm' (7.400). The 'bringing forth' of the sixth day becomes, in a bravura display of baroque art, a powerful and vigorous scene of parturition:

> The earth . . . straight
> Opening her fertile womb teemed at a birth
> Innumerous living creatures, perfect forms,
> Limbed and full grown . . .
>
> (7.453–6)

Let us be clear: the procreative riot in which Milton conceptualises and represents the process of creation is certainly implicit in the Genesis account and explicit in the recurrent refrain of 'Be fruitful and multiply' (1:22, 28). Milton retains and foregrounds it, both as a celebration of the generative principle (in a sense Book 7 is his *Primavera*) and as an explanation in humanly comprehensible terms of the relatively slow implementation of a divine policy which could have been instituted instantaneously, given the physical limitlessness of the Godhead.

Nature shares humankind's imperative to replicate itself; it shares, too, humankind's guilt. In an early poem, his ode 'On the Morning of Christ's Nativity', Milton contrasts Nature's consciousness of her sinfulness with the true innocence of the incarnate Christ:

> [Nature] woos the gentle air
>   To hide her guilty front with innocent snow,
> And on her naked shame,
> Pollute with sinful blame,
>   The saintly veil of maiden white to throw,
> Confounded, that her maker's eyes
> Should look so near upon her foul deformities
>
> (lines 38–44, *Poems*, 102–3)

The poem rehearses the rich paradox that the Son made the created world, embodied in the personification of Nature, and now is born into that world as its youngest neonate. *Paradise Lost* offers a prequel to those events, in its account of the impact of the fall on creation.

As Eve takes the forbidden fruit:

> Earth felt the wound, and nature from her seat
> Sighing through all her works gave signs of woe,
> That all was lost.'
>
> (9.782–4)

As she returns to Adam, who has been weaving a garland for her, he releases it '[f]rom his slack hand'; down it drops, 'and all the faded roses shed' (9.892–3). The reader (and perhaps especially any reader shaped by the European consciousness, dominant since the Romantic era, of the inherent purity and beneficence of the natural world) may feel prompted to object to the logic of such events. How can it be *right* that the decision of (one member of) one species should so blight the well-being of all of creation? Why has the Godhead ordered creation to permit this? (That one species should thus derange global systems may seem true but not right to those nurtured in the ecologically sensitive ideological climate of the late twentieth century; as we have seen and shall see, Milton is the greenest of poets.)

Justification of the global impact of Eve's and then Adam's sins is largely carried at a level deeper and more tacit than that of logical exposition. The life of Adam and Eve, at every stage, has been represented as intimately and inextricably involved in the life of their planet. This is the secondary effect of Milton's representation of the process of creation as analogous to sexual reproduction; Adam and Eve, persistently charged with the responsibility of procreation, and the teemingly fertile world, obey the same life rhythms and the same sexual impulses and imperatives. Again, the world has been so much with them; Adam first awoke and spoke to the created world; he has named the species; the world in its various manifestations attended and celebrated his marriage to Eve; nightly it strewed the marriage bed with 'roses, which the morn repaired' (4.773); it has fed them, and, in the form of 'the unwieldly elephant . . . with [h]is lithe proboscis' (4.345–7), it has even entertained them. That it should share their fate and their taint appears convincing at those older, deeper levels of understanding where notions like sympathetic magic have their wellsprings.

But the Miltonic consciousness synthesises the older perceptions with the explicitness of the newer climate of scientificity. Before the fall, the climate had been stable, constant and equable; now it is subject to change, and he represents this change in terms of one of two alternative hypotheses (Miltonic cosmology makes sense to the reader whether he or she operates from geocentric or heliocentric assumptions, as Fowler best explains). Before the fall, the ecliptic plane, that is, the plane apparently described by the sun around the earth, and the equatorial plane, that is, the plane around the centre of the earth, coincided. Thus the sun's apparent route was unchangingly around the equator, irrespective of the time of the year. The effect of this is to ensure that, throughout the world, a perpetual (and palpably vernal) equinox obtained; day and night are each twelve hours, everywhere. The fall breaks the coincidence of the ecliptic and equatorial planes, thus admitting seasonal variations, with the cold of winter and the scorching heat of summer. If we assume that the cosmic system is heliocentric, then we are invited to conceptualise this seasonal change as a consequence of earth's axis being pushed out of true, so that the equatorial plane no longer corresponds with the ecliptic plane defined by the sun's apparent movement:

> Some say [the Father] bid his angels turn askance
> The poles of earth twice ten degrees and more
> From the sun's axle . . .

> (10.668–70)

Alternatively, if the universe is really geocentric, then a relocation of the orbital plane of the sun must be the explanation for seasonal fluctuation:

>   some say the sun
> Was bid turn reins from the equinoctial road
> Like distant breadth to Taurus with the Seven
> Atlantic Sisters, and the Spartan Twins
> Up to the tropic Crab; thence down amain
> By Leo and the Virgin and the Scales,
> As deep as Capricorn . . .

> (10.671–7)

That is, his course varies an equal distance from the equator, northwards, at the northern summer solstice, to the Tropic of

Cancer ('the tropic Crab'), and southwards, at the northern winter solstice, to the Tropic of Capricorn ('[a]s deep as Capricorn').

Whatever the mechanism (and postlapsarian people are no wiser than the puzzled prelapsarian Adam on this point), the effect produces many an 'adverse blast' (10.701), numbing cold and scorching heat. Milton challenges his readers, surely one or other of these cosmic shifts must have happened,

> else how had the world
> Inhabited, though sinless, more than now,
> Avoided pinching cold and scorching heat?
>
> (689–91)

If the reader has a better explanation, he or she is welcome to advance it; Milton's doubts that it will work, however. Whatever happened, the world at once became much less hospitable to all its inhabitants. But note that Milton's account assigns to an angelic task force the duties of inflicting the new climatic irregularities, rather than to the Son, who had formerly created the universe and had, effortlessly, undertaken the celestial alignments which formerly obtained. Again, whereas the Son had created the world with effortless elegance, its unhinging calls for hard work: they 'with labour pushed/Oblique the centric globe' (10.670–1).

The need for clothing is a matter of practicality as well as newly acquired shame, and the kindness of the Son in anticipation provides it, as the Genesis account states (3:21), though Milton is as uncertain as other exegetes had been about whether the skins were sloughed off like snakeskin or from beasts that had been slain (10.217–19).

Certainly, very quickly, there is death enough within Paradise. An ecological system which had previously been vegetarian admits the roles of predators and prey:

> Beast now with beast gan war, and fowl with fowl,
> And fish with fish; to graze the herb all leaving,
> Devoured each other; nor stood much in awe
> Of man, but fled him, or with countenance grim
> Glared on him passing: these were from without
> The growing miseries, which Adam saw
> Already in part . . .
>
> (10.710–16)

Milton perhaps overstates the issue – or is this a view from within the gloomy subjectivity of Adam?: after all, some species in the food chain remain herbivores. Adam registers, too, a new threat to humankind, in that some of those creatures which once had entertained him now look at him as potential food.

'Earth felt the wound': indeed so. Milton's depictions of the creation of the world are of a living system intimately, almost humanly, connected with the life of humankind; the fall of Adam and Eve reverberates not only through the generations of their offspring more widely, to the system that supports all species in all places. Perhaps only Wordsworth among the major English poets so fully understood the interconnectedness of things.

NOTES

1.   Regina Schwartz, *Remembering and Repeating: Biblical Creation in* Paradise Lost (Cambridge and New York: Cambridge University Press, 1988), especially Chapter 1. For a valuable early account, see A. B. Chambers, 'Chaos in *Paradise Lost*', *Journal of the History of Ideas*, 24 (1963), pp. 55–84.

2.   Arnold Williams, *The Common Expositor: An Account of the Commentaries on Genesis 1527–1633* (Chapel Hill, NC: University of North Carolina Press, 1948).

Chapter 5

The English Epic

NEOCLASSICISM AND THE ENGLISH EPIC

'That Milton used classical models for *Paradise Lost* may be the stalest news in Milton criticism': thus Blessington begins his purposeful study of Milton's debt to the classical epic.[1] Indeed, Milton's relationship to Homer and Virgil obsessed his earliest critics and commentators. Among English vernacular poets, he attracted rather more critical attention in the late seventeenth and early eighteenth centuries than any other except Shakespeare; the emphasis of much of this critical effort lay was placed on demonstrating that classical lineage. Patrick Hume's annotations of 1695 note the parallels between Milton and classical models, and the work is consolidated in Thomas Newton's edition of 1749 and thereafter absorbed into the growing corpus of Miltonic annotation.[2] Joseph Addison's eighteen essays in *The Spectator* in 1712 offer the most influential account of *Paradise Lost* within the perspective of English neoclassicism. For Addison, that active classical intertext offers a special kind of pleasure unavailable to the less educated, who may nevertheless enjoy the poem in purely English terms:

> I must take notice, that *Milton* is every where full of Hints, and sometimes literal Translations, taken from the greatest of the *Greek* and *Latin* Poets. But this I may reserve for a Discourse by itself, because I would not break the Thread of these Speculations that are designed for *English* Readers, with such Reflections as would be of no use but to the Learned.[3]

Addison's primary agenda is elegantly simple: it is to assert the status of Milton's poem by demonstrating that it satisfies formal criteria derived both directly from Homer and Virgil and indirectly from classical and neoclassical critics of Homer and Virgil, pre-eminently Aristotle and Longinus. The genre characteristics or markers which he identifies and, in a sense, celebrates are formal aspects of plot, character and incident, certain linguistic practices which differentiate epic discourse from quotidian expression, and above all the 'sublimity' of sentiment which is the hallmark of epic in Longinan terms. At the outset of the eighteen-essay series which contains the major part of his commentary on Milton, he defines the terms of his enquiry: 'I shall . . . examine [*Paradise Lost*] by the Rules of Epic Poetry, and see whether it falls short of the *Iliad* or *Aeneid* in the Beauties which are essential to that kind of Writing' (*Spectator*, 2.539). Of course, he finds, for the most part, that it does not fall short. Addison writes over half a century after Milton, and the differences between the cultural configuration in which he operated and that of the 1660s must be brought sharply into focus. Addison writes after the victory of neoclassical aesthetic ideology; Milton writes in the heat of that cultural revolution. By the 1710s, in literature as in several other cultural domains, neoclassicism's twin claims, that the cultural triumphs of the ancient world constitute both touchstone and model of contemporary achievement, and that contemporary, vernacular art can purposefully accept the challenge of those ancient models, had achieved a wide acceptance. In the 1660s, such claims are advanced, not as sure orthodoxies, but as shibboleths of a new and fragile cultural epoch.

Addison writes as though Milton's purpose had been to meet the polemical exigencies of the neoclassical case. Parallels with Homer afford just the evidence he needs:

> The greater Incidents [in *Paradise Lost*] . . . are not only set off by being shown in the same Light, with several of the same Nature in *Homer*, but by that means may be also guarded against the Cavils of the Tasteless or Ignorant.
>
> (*Spectator*, 3.312)

Not only does Milton's achievement demonstrate that classical standards may be met in contemporary (or, at least, recent) vernacular writing but also it vindicates English as a medium for the highest literary creativity. Milton becomes incorporated in the cultural nationalism deeply inscribed in Addison's criticism. His epic is 'a Work which does an Honour to the *English* Nation' (*Spectator*, 3.391). Revealingly, at one point when issues of comparison with

Tasso emerge naturally in Addison's argument, he actually shies off with the words 'I would not perplex my Reader with such Quotations, as might do more Honour to the *Italian* than the *English* Poet' (*Spectator*, 3.392). Indeed, in the later eighteenth century so firmly does Milton become rooted as the dominant figure in the canon of English narrative poetry that to criticise him is to invite an accusation of unpatriotic activity. Johnson, far fonder of his country than of Milton, recognises the problem and negotiates it carefully in his *Life* of the poet, as Hunter has noted.[4] Fittingly, when English culture selects its first home-grown literary icon its choice is for one who may be perceived as exemplar of English neoclassicism.

More recent critics have recognised the inadequacy of Addison's rather undynamic model for Milton's place in the western literary tradition. Hunter[5] and Fowler in his edition of Milton have recognised the essentially dynamic nature of Milton's adoption of the epic genre in English vernacular literature.

Milton's task was much harder than even the grandiose idiom of Addison recognises. Throughout the high Renaissance in England a delicate relationship had been negotiated with the culture of the classical world. Mere imitation of classical models and cultural practices carried with it the taint of bourgeois scholasticism. The courtly idiom, more Italianate than classical, handled the classical models with a discerning detachment and distance. Shakespeare, subtly alert to the complexities of his own class and cultural position, adopts a deeply ambivalent stance. Like Ben Jonson, the real founding father of English literary classicism, he is drawn to the dramatisation of Roman history, although his own use of Latin source materials is relatively amateurish in comparison with the historiographical rigour of Jonson's *Catiline* or *Sejanus*. But only with care does he adopt Latinate neologisms in non-comic writing. Perhaps his most famously Latinate lines are from a soliloquy of Macbeth: 'this my hand will rather/The multitudinous seas incarnadine'; but, as others have noted, he immediately softens the grand phrase with a simple English gloss: 'Making the green one red' (Act 2. Scene 2.59–60). Classical imitation (rather than his own intricately mediated relationship with classical culture) appears the mark of the uncourtly pedant. Whatever connection the figure of the schoolmaster Holofernes in *Love's Labour's Lost* may have with specific figures who were Shakespeare's contemporaries, he represents the unacceptable, aspiring-bourgeois face of English neoclassicism. He is idiolectally differentiated by gratuitious Latinisms: 'The deer was, as you know – *sanguis* – in blood, ripe as the pomewater [a kind of apple] who now hangeth like a jewel in the ear of *caelo*, the sky.' As his social equal, the curate Nathaniel, observes, 'Truly . . . the epithets are sweetly varied, like a scholar at the least' (4.2). (Note, though, that even for Holofernes's classical borrowings Shakespeare introduces a vernacular gloss.)

The high–Renaissance uncertainty about the relationship English culture should strike with the culture of the ancient world finds expression in the term 'ink–horn', first used as an epithet for gratuitously bookish language in the mid–sixteenth century and frequently bandied about in the sometimes acrimonious exchanges between Elizabethan and Jacobean writers (*OED* s.v. 'Ink–horn,' 2.b.; see also 'Inkhornism,' 'Inkhornist', and 'Inkhornize'). It was an anxiety which persisted strongly into Milton's own age, and it characterises some of the comments Milton makes in his controversial prose. Thus in his *Colasterion* (1645) he ridicules his enemy William Prynne's affectation of the word 'subitane', which he has coined from the Latin *subitaneus* as an alternative to the long-native 'sudden', and he takes issue with the author of *Eikon Basilike*, ostensibly the late Charles I, for borrowing from Greek the word 'Demogogue', which he terms a 'Goblin word': 'the King by his leave cannot coine English as he could Money.'[6] There is a particular frisson in the latter sally since Milton, himself (like Shakespeare) the son of a bourgeois, lays the charge of pedantic affectation against his late King.

But of course very many terms were borrowed into English from Latin and, to a less extent, from Greek, in the sixteenth and early seventeenth centuries. Such words were as much a part of the English Milton wrote as they are of late twentieth-century English, and though they were readily naturalised and became involved in the normal processes of word formation from the established word stock, many remained recognisably cognate with Latin and Greek words. However, the meaning of many words changed rapidly in the late-seventeenth and early-eighteenth centuries, so that eighteenth-century commentators on Milton sometimes misperceived his then quite normal English usage of a word of Latin origin as in some sense a 'Latinism', a consciously atavistic use of a word of classical origin in a signification once current in Latin but not current in English.

Modern scholarship has done much to purge the commentary tradition of hordes of such 'ghost Latinisms', to use Fowler's excellent term (Fowler, p. 14), and Fowler himself has played a signal part.

What emerges is a much more delicate sense of the ways in which
Milton, carefully, ties the characteristic idiom of his poem to the
idiom of classical authors in such a way as to indicate a continuity
of discourse, but without compromising the essential Englishness of
what he is doing.

In *Paradise Lost*, sometimes the neologism provokes pertinent
recollection of the Virgilian intertext, as in

> him [Satan] round
> A globe of fiery seraphim enclosed
> With bright emblazonry, and horrent arms.

> (2.511–13)

'Horrent,' 'bristling,' suggests a Virgilian echo, *mille rapit densos
acie atque horrentibus hastis* (*Aeneid*, 10.178) ('he hurries on a thousand
men, densely packed, in the battle formation and with bristling
spears'). As such it prepares the reader for the section very shortly
afterwards which rehearses the classical epic topos of the heroic
games, albeit (and significantly) played by fallen angels. Again,
when Milton ascribes to Adam 'hyacinthine locks' (4.301), the
informed reader recognises an echo of Homer's description of
Odysseus's 'locks like the hyacinthine flower' (*Odyssey*, 6.231),
which functions as a neat marker of Milton's cultural orientation
and lightly links his epic to the classical model through a com-
munity of heroic attributes.[7]

I suspect that English literary neoclassicism was marked by a
narrow subset of the English language constituted by a small
number of terms and idioms borrowed from Latin and Greek.
A number of words used apparently gratuitously by Milton are
shared with earlier neoclassicists. Consider, for example, the word
'clang', used of the cry of birds. It had been used in English to mean
'the sound of a trumpet', which is another signification of the Latin
word *clangor*, but, as Fowler notes, it was used of birds by George
Chapman, Elizabethan and Jacobean translator of Homer, to render
the line 'By her clange they knew . . . it was a hern [that is, heron]'
(*Iliad*, 10.244). Again, 'in procinct,' that is, 'ready, prepared,' can
be perceived as a perhaps slightly Holofernesian imitation of *in
procinctu*: 'War he [Abdiel] perceived, war in procinct' (*Paradise Lost*
6.19), but there is an analogue in Chapman's *Iliad* (12.89).

Lexical aspects of English literary neoclassicism await a fuller
account. What is better established is the cultural significance of

Milton's prosodic innovation. Though the Earl of Surrey had experimented in the mid-sixteenth century with unrhymed verse in his translation of Books 2 and 4 of the *Aeneid*, rhyme had remained the norm for English narrative poetry, even translations, such as those of Chapman, of Greek or Latin classics. Revolutionarily, Milton opts for unrhymed verse. His reasons may well have been complex, and I have argued elsewhere that eschewing the exigencies of rhyme may well have been an element in the prose-like elaboration of his syntax.[8] Evidently his choice was felt to require some explanation. The early issues of the first edition of *Paradise Lost* (1667) were published, somewhat starkly, without prefatory material. But for the second issue of 1668, as for subsequent issues, the publisher included not only the prose arguments, which later became distributed to the head of each constituent book, but also a short essay on the verse. Both, we may assume, are the work of the poet; and both, presumably, represent some response to the puzzlement of his earliest readers, puzzlement in part at the difficulty of following the broken chronology of the narrative and in part at the surprise of finding an English narrative poem without rhyme. The essay, the belligerent idiom of which is profoundly redolent of Milton's controversial prose, makes two points, which together indicate the difficult orientation of the poet's neoclassicising impulse. Blank verse, he says, has been used in other modern vernacular literatures, not least in what he offers as elevated English achievement, 'our best *English* [his italics] Tragedies'. His first point, though, is that this is traditional English 'Heroic Verse', that is, presumably, iambic pentameter, brought into line with the practice of the ranking classical models: it is 'without Rime, as that of *Homer*, in *Greek*, and of *Virgil* in *Latin*'. Rhyme in narrative poetry is dismissed as an unnecessary accretion of 'a barbarous Age', and, in a flourish which discloses both a political subtext (Milton reforming English prosody, as once he had sought to reform the English church and constitution, back to a primitive pristine state) and a neoclassical agenda, he speaks of his epic as 'an example set, the first in *English*, of ancient liberty recover'd to Heroic Poem from the troublesom and modern bondage of Rimeing'.[9]

Evidently the shockingness and the cultural challenge of Milton's prosodic innovation continued to exercise the publisher, for in the second edition (1674) it is addressed again in the commendatory

poems which are affixed to the epic for the first time. The poem
which is usually attributed to Samuel Barrow, with a fulsomeness
perhaps less surprising in neo-Latin, rather than vernacular poetry,
foregrounds the way in which Milton's epic claims the niche held
by Homer and Virgil:

> Cedite Romani *Scriptores, cedite* Graii
> > *Et quos fama recens vel celebravit anus.*
> *Haec quicunque leget tantum cecinesse putabit*
> > Maeonidem *ranas,* Virgilium *culices.*[10]

> [Yield writers of Rome, yield writers of Greece and those whom
> fame, recent or ancient, has celebrated. Who reads this poem will
> think Maeonides sang of frogs, Virgil of gnats.][11]

Addison would have applauded the cultural nationalism; but note
that Barrow does not argue that Milton equals the classical models;
rather, he so surpasses them that their epics are but mock-epics
by comparison with the authentic and – as the rest of the com-
mendatory poem makes clear – *Christian* epic.

The other commendatory poem is the rather more famous verse
by Andrew Marvell. His emphasis rests very largely on the issue of
rhyme, with a mannered reflexivity remarking on his own rhymed
celebration of Milton's superior blank verse:

> I too transported by the Mode [of rhyme] offend,
> And while I meant to Praise thee must Commend.
> Thy Verse created like thy Theme sublime,
> In Number, Weight, and Measure, needs not Rhime.[12]

Again, interestingly, Marvell, while celebrating the classicism of
Milton's prosody, elevates his poem over others by the sublimity
of its Christian theme. Evidently, the prefatory material negotiates
a subtle and sophisticated relationship between Miltonic neo-
classicism and ancient practice.

Within the poem Milton's own comments about his cultural
agenda speak of tension and challenge, rather than simple imitation.
Not only does he seek to establish epic in vernacular English, but
also he seeks to redefine the nature of epic in Christian terms.

Perhaps the sharpest statement of the issues comes late in the
poem, in the invocation to Book 9, when the reader is already
deeply involved in the experience of the new epic idiom. At
once Milton explicitly subordinates pagan to Christian epic and

rehearses his anxiety about the portability of the genre to his own culture. He is:

> Not sedulous by nature to indite
> Wars, hitherto the only argument
> Heroic deemed . . .

(9.27–9)

Such stuff, like the feasts, games and tournaments of classical and Renaissance, chivalric epic, do not constitute the proper material for Christian contemplation. For the Christian, not outward boldness but spiritual courage make the fit subject for high art. It is an ambitious flourish, this attempt to reappraise the hierarchy of literary subject matter and literary form in such a way as to assert the values of the mind, and of the internal struggle of the godly, over the palpable and rather spectacular achievement of those who are traditionally 'heroic deemed':

> Me of these
> Nor skilled nor studious, higher argument
> Remains, sufficient of it self to raise
> That name [i.e., heroic] . . .

(9.41–4)

Indeed, his poem works persistently against echoes of Homeric and Virgilian epic, to assert the superiority of his newly Christianised epic aesthetic. The wars are relegated to recollection; the games played out by the fallen angels; centre stage and direct narration of action are left to the internal struggles of Adam and Eve, their fall, and their spiritual regeneration.

Against this vaulting assertion of his epic's status over the classical masters comes the qualification that the state of contemporary English culture (and other factors) may preclude his success. He can redeem the concept of the heroic for Christianity:

> unless an age too late, or cold
> Climate, or years damp my intended wing
> Depressed, and much they may, if all be mine,
> Not hers who brings it nightly to my ear.

(9.44–7)

As we have noted, his notion of the inspiring muse is not to be lightly dismissed as a mere neoclassical trapping, for Milton has carefully established her characteristics at the outset of the poem, equating her, in effect, with the Holy Ghost, the inspirer of Moses in the Pentateuchal writing on which *Paradise Lost* is largely based (see Chapter 1). As such, Milton carefully privileges his muse over Virgil's and Homer's. While the severity of his task of inserting into English literary tradition an epic poem which in most senses matches the formal characteristics of classical epic is acknowledged, he simultaneously asserts both his transcendence in purpose, subject and inspiration of the classical masters and his right to adjust the epic genre to fit the values of his higher spiritual concerns.

THE SYNTAX OF *PARADISE LOST*

So far I have touched on one familiar proposition relating to the style of *Paradise Lost*, namely, that its lexis is in some respects un-English, and I have argued that, while Milton adopts a number of cultural/linguistic markers common among vernacular neo-classicists of the English Renaissance, that 'charge' (it is always latterly advanced in denigratory fashion) is without foundation.

Another supposedly un-English element can also be dismissed: Milton's syntactic preferences are merely commonplace within the norms of English vernacular practice. What makes them remarkable, however, is that they accord with the norms of English prose, rather than English poetry.[13]

If the sentences of *Paradise Lost* are compared with narrative poems by other seventeenth-century English writers, then the guess of most modern readers can be confirmed: Milton's sentences are considerably longer, on average, than those of his contemporaries. They contain more words, more syllables, and more clauses. They are more complex in the sense that they contain a higher proportion of subordinated material. Very frequently in *Paradise Lost* subordinate clauses depend on main clauses, and those subordinate clauses, in turn, support other clauses which are subordinate to them. The subordinate clauses which are dependent on subordinate clauses may support yet further subordinate clauses, and so on through a long hierarchy of dependence. Some clauses may support a plurality of subordinate clauses.

Although such complex sentences are commonplace in *Paradise Lost* (and in some other poems by Milton), they are very rare in narrative poems by Sir Richard Fanshawe, by John Dryden, and by Abraham Cowley (authors selected for exhaustive statistical comparison in my earlier study). However, if one turns to the controversial prose written by Milton and by others engaged in the polemical exchanges of the English Civil War, one encounters many such sentences (both in Milton and among his contemporaries). The typical sentence structure of Milton's prose is scarcely to be differentiated from many contemporary prose writers; the typical sentence structure of *Paradise Lost*, though it is in many ways analogous to the typical sentence structure of mid-seventeenth-century prose, is unparalleled among mid-seventeenth-century narrative poets. Thus, the experience of reading *Paradise Lost* is in this respect unique (and uniquely difficult) for the modern reader.

Let us consider those analogies with the syntactical preference of Milton's prose by analysing a sentence we have considered already in terms of its ideological significance (in Chapter 1). This is a distinctively Miltonic sentence from *Paradise Lost*:

> [S]o shall the world go on,
> To good malignant, to bad men benign,
> Under her own weight groaning, till the day
> Appear of respiration to the just,
> And vengeance to the wicked, at return
> Of him so lately promised to thy aid
> The woman's seed, obscurely then foretold,
> Now amplier known thy saviour and thy Lord,
> Last in the clouds from heaven to be revealed
> In glory of the Father, to dissolve
> Satan with his perverted world, then raise
> From the conflagrant mass, purged and refined,
> New heavens, new earth, ages of endless date
> Founded in righteousness and peace and love
> To bring forth fruits joy and eternal bliss.

(12.537–51)

The main clause is '[S]o shall the world go on,/To good malignant, to bad men benign'. This directly supports a clause (for these purposes I regard participial phrases as clauses), describing the action of the world: 'Under her own weight groaning'. Complex syntactical structures often contain an element of ambiguity or uncertainty, and the next clause, 'till the day/Appear of respiration to the just,/And vengeance to the wicked, at return/Of him', could be regarded as defining either the continuity of the world or the world's groaning; that is, it could depend on the first clause or on the second. However one perceives it, it evidently supports four subordinate clauses in turn, each describing an aspect of the revelation of the Son: first, 'so lately promised to thy aid'; second, 'obscurely then foretold'; third, '[n]ow amplier known thy saviour and thy Lord'; and finally, '[l]ast in the clouds from heaven to be revealed/In glory of the Father'. That last clause supports further subordination, expatiation on the purpose of the Son's final manifestation: 'to dissolve/Satan with his perverted world' and 'then raise/From the conflagrant mass . . . /New heavens, new earth, ages of endless date'. That 'conflagrant mass' is briefly qualified by two very short participial clauses, each of one word: 'purged' and 'refined'. The new heavens and new earth, however, are more fully described, again in a participial phrase, '[f]ounded in righteousness and peace and love'. That in turn supports the final clause, indicating purpose, '[t]o bring forth fruits of joy and eternal bliss'.

So what? The formal analysis of literary texts in syntactical terms is often dismissed in the current critical period. However, I offer two rejoinders.

The first is that appreciating the complex structure of Miltonic sentences can disclose numerous points of local brilliance within *Paradise Lost*. Here, for example, the reader's concentration, taxed to its limit, struggles towards that final clause, dependent as it is, at sixth remove, on the main clause with which the sentence opened: '[t]o bring forth fruits joy and eternal bliss'. As Fowler observes, 'fruits' echoes the opening lines of the poem, 'Of man's first disobedience, and the fruit/Of that forbidden tree' (12.551n), and, as Ricks has noted, 'fruit(s)', in both literal and more metaphorical significations, recurs in interesting ways throughout the poem.[14] Here, in the sentence which concludes Michael's long account of mankind's prospects in the fallen world, a gloomy account finally relieved by the triumphant but remote vision of the Second Coming, it occurs for the last time. The final fruits of that disobedient fruit–eating, primarily thanks to Christ's atonement, but secondarily thanks to the godly's own perseverance, are indeed 'joy and bliss', but they are achieved at length and after struggle, much as that final clause, which resolves the problems the poem has posed, is arrived at only after the reader has struggled to comprehend a sentence of awesome complexity.

Joy and bliss are arrived at with a final understanding of the sentence.

Secondly, the syntax of Milton's prose, which remained remarkably stable over his long career as polemicist, bears striking similarities to the example from *Paradise Lost*. Consider this wholly typical sentence, from his earliest political pamphlet, *Of Reformation* (1641):

> But they contrary that by the impairing and diminution of the true *Faith*, the distresses and servitude of their *Countrey* aspire to high *Dignity*, *Rule* and *Promotion* here, after a shamefull end in this *Life* (which *God* grant them) shall be thrown downe eternally into the *darkest* and *deepest Gulfe* of HELL, where under the *despightfull countroule*, the trample and spurne of all the other *Damned*, that in the anguish of their *Torture* shall have no other ease then to exercise a *Raving* and *Bestiall Tyranny* over them as their *Slaves* and *Negro's*, they shall remaine in that plight for ever, the *basest*, the *lowermost*, the *most dejected*, most *underfoot*, and *downe-trodden Vassals* of *Perdition*.
>
> (*CPW*, 1.616–17)

The sentence begins with a main clause: 'But they . . . after a shamefull end . . . shall be thrown downe eternally into . . . HELL' (Milton is talking about the prelatical party – discussed in Chapter 6 – who will be punished at the Second Coming while the godly are rewarded with joy and bliss). That main clause contains within it a subordinate clause defining the 'they' ('that by impairing . . . *Promotion* here') and another subordinate clause telling us more about the end in this life which Milton would wish them ('which *God* grant them'). The sentence continues with a further subordinate clause dependent on the main clause and this time describing the conditions which await his enemies in hell: 'where they shall remaine in that plight for ever, the most . . . *downe-trodden Vassals* of *Perdition*'. That subordinate clause supports another subordinate clause concerning the other inhabitants of hell and their relationship to the bishops' party: 'that in the anguish . . . over them as their *Slaves* and *Negro's*'. This sentence, too, concludes a passage (in fact it closes the much more immediate millenarian vision with which the whole pamphlet ends), and it has an exultant, vituperative quality which renders it a resounding conclusion, though one arrived at with some effort.

In generating sentences in his poetry which are analogous to sentences in his prose (and in other serious prose of the mid-seventeenth century) Milton frequently achieves numerous local felicities. The general point, however, is that he produces in his verse a medium capable of carrying the larger arguments, the elevated rhetoric, the complex intricacies of consequence and resolution and qualification which contemporaneously occurred only in the medium of prose. As we have seen, Milton's verse engages difficult issues in intellectually rigorous terms, issues right at the edge of avant-guardist speculation; he may engage such issues because he has generated a poetry capable of carrying the syntactical complexities of elevated prose.

It may seem that the sorts of sentences considered above are in some ways Latinate. Certainly, they share some of the grandness of scope and complexity which characterises the style of Ciceronian oratory. However, syntactically, they are generated wholly by familiar native procedures for subordination; syntactically, they are wholly English. Clauses are appended to clauses using the same features as Milton's contemporaries used. The clausal order is completely vernacular. Simply, Milton in his poetry often writes the long, complex sentences which characterise the serious English prose of his age.

NARRATIVE STRUCTURE

Though the second edition of *Paradise Lost*, published in 1674, contained only very minor changes to the words of the poem as it first appeared in 1667, it allowed a major restructuring of the book division. The first edition was in 10 books, the second was in 12; the change was effected by dividing Book 7 of the first edition to make Books 7 and 8 and by dividing Book 10 of the first edition to make Books 11 and 12. The primary advantage would seem to relate to Milton's neoclassicism. The *Aeneid*, the classical poem *Paradise Lost* most closely resembles, has 12 books. There may also have been advantages in terms of the symbolic structure; Fowler has argued that the placing of four invocations at the start of Books 1, 3, 7, and 9 (second edition), rather than 1, 3, 7, and 8 (first edition) works as a structuring device (though the placing in the first edition is also tractable to justification and interpretation). But the second edition constitutes a clear degradation in terms of number symbolism in that minor additions to the text nudge the image of the Son entering into the Father's chariot away from its exact point of centrality by four and a half lines. Much more significantly, Røstvig has recently argued that the first edition manifests a series of complex symbolic symmetries which have been lost in the second.[15] The issues remain controversial, though Røstvig's argument in favour of the first edition as the structurally superior is powerfully persuasive.

The ordering of events within the poem poses fascinating interpretative problems. At its simplest Milton's decision to eschew simple chronology constitutes another neoclassical gesture. Virgil had begun his narrative not with the fall of Troy but with Aeneas's arrival in Carthage, rushing into events, and the earlier disaster is related by Aeneas as a protracted analepsis or flashback. Similarly, *Paradise Lost* begins with the re-animation of the fallen angels, rather than with their overthrow, just as we have Aeneas's arrival before the events which dislocated him from his home. Again, the reader sees Adam and Eve living in Paradise before the account of its formation. In this nesting of earlier events within the chronological sequence Milton may be perceived as demonstrating control of one of the genre characteristics of classical epic.

But other, subtler arguments may be entertained. Milton's poem is structurally and thematically focussed on the earth and on the human struggles of Adam and Eve and their descendants; we, the humans, are its principal concerns, rather than the struggle of Satan and the angels. Though paradoxically the middle of the poem is dominated by events in heaven, the structure places the emphasis on the human and terrestrial plane. Over Books 1, 2 and 3, the human race is anticipatively discussed, in heaven as well as hell. Over Books 9 to 12 human figures, including the human, incarnate Son, dominate the stage, and the work leads out from the paradisal experience to the everyday struggles of the godly reader.

In part the ordering of events also relates to the argument of the poem. Milton's primary purpose, on his assertion to 'assert eternal providence,/And justify the ways of God to men' (1.25-6), requires a quasi-forensic presentation of evidence. The reader needs to be convinced that Adam and Eve know all that is necessary for their Fall to be justified and for them to be denied a plea of ignorance by way of mitigation. Hence that revealing comment in the headnote to Book 5: 'God to render man inexcusable sends Raphael to admonish him of his obedience, of his free estate, of his enemy near at hand' (see above, Chapter 3). By nesting the narration of the war in heaven within Raphael's instruction of Adam and Eve we witness it and confirm God's justice. We know what they know and we know that they know it.

Similarly, the preview of world history which Michael vouchsafes to Adam allows us to share the learning process with him. First we see, then we interpret, and we are corrected and learn from the error. Thus, in the third vision Adam sees the grandchildren of Cain engaged in a civilisation of some luxury and sophistication (11.556–97). After the horror of the first two visions Adam (and perhaps the reader) takes pleasure and relief from the change, and Adam exclaims,

> True opener of mine eyes, prime angel blest,
> Much better seems this vision, and more hope
> Of peaceful days portends, than those two past;
> Those were of hate and death, or pain much worse,
> Here nature seems fulfilled in all her ends.
>
> (11.598–602)

This allows Michael to caution him and us with a stern moral:

> Judge not what is best
> By pleasure, though to nature seeming meet,
> Created, as thou art, to nobler end
> Holy and pure, conformity divine.
>
> (11.603–06)

The stern warning cautions the godly Adam poised to leave Paradise and the godly Christian contemplating the seductive luxuries of the revived Stuart court; the devil has some excellent tunes, but they must be resisted.

Such small-scale pedagogic effects arguably have an equivalent in the larger design of the poem. It is often observed that Milton's decision to place the dynamic image of Satan in the opening books lures the ingenuous into an inappropriate sympathy from which they eventually recoil all the wiser for the experience. As Fish puts it in his influential account of the reader's response to the poem:

> The wariness these encounters with demonic attraction make us feel is part of the larger pattern in which we are taught the hardest of all lesssons, distrust of our own abilities and perceptions.[16]

I have some reservations about the postulated notion of the naive reader of *Paradise Lost*, but I certainly agree that the introduction of Satan before the Godhead contributes considerably to the expressive power of the poem. Milton's persistent strategy in representing God is to invite us to consider the awesome power of angels and then to posit a being that far transcends that power. The opening books establish the scale of angelic existence, in their number and in their energy. But Satan's dynamic courage, fully realised in his journey through Chaos, is made to seem trivial at the opening of Book 3, where the Father and the Son watch him with amusement and contempt; they can look on him, though he cannot look on them. Just as God uses Satan in his moral test on Adam and Eve, so Milton uses him in establishing the transcendence of the Godhead.

But Milton's poem is at most only transitorily dialogic. When the fallen are allowed a seductive voice, correction follows soon from the narrator. Milton shows us Satan's energy, but pulls us up sharply with the encounter with Sin and Death, whose grotesque images dispel Satanism's apparent charms. Again, Satan's tragic meditations of the poignancy of his mission to destroy Adam and Eve's life in Paradise is quickly dashed by the narrator's dismissal of 'necessity,/The tyrant's plea' (4.393–4; see above, Chapter 2).

Milton invests much in establishing the authority of the narrative voice. As we have seen, it is equated with the Holy Spirit, with divine inspiration; the poet becomes God's voice, God's scribe, in the manner of Moses accepting and transmitting the Pentateuch. The narrator is vividly established, in middle age, blind, surrounded by his enemies, but distinguished and privileged in the nightly visitation of the holy muse. Moreover, the poet oversees his narration of world history as God controls and views the events of that history; divine providence is matched by narratorial control. Thus the poem begins with a sentence which contains the whole span of the human experience, past, present and future, and associates the poet with the unique task of describing that experience:

> Of man's first disobedience, and the fruit
> Of that forbidden tree, whose mortal taste
> Brought death into the world, and all our woe,
> With loss of Eden, till one greater man
> Restore us, and regain the blissful seat,
> Sing heavenly Muse, that on the secret top
> Of Oreb, or of Sinai, didst inspire
> That shepherd, who first taught the chosen seed,

In the beginning how the heavens and earth
Rose out of chaos: or if Sion hill
Delight thee more, and Siloa's brook that flowed
Fast by the oracle of God; I thence
Invoke thy aid to my adventurous song,
That with no middle flight intends to soar
Above the Aonian mount, while it pursues
Things unattempted yet in prose or rhyme.

(1.1–16)

Thus events from 4004 BC ('loss of Eden') and from early in the first century AD (the Incarnation and Atonement) are linked with the millennium; and the recounting of those events by Milton in 1667 is linked, through the transhistorical operation of the Christian muse, with the Pentateuchal narration of Moses. The effect of the passage is two-fold. It defines the narrator's voice as authoritative, and it asserts a complete control over the narrative line, despite the fact that it relates in part to prophetic events and despite the fact that it covers at least six millennia. Thus the narrator takes control; if he temporarily allows other voices, including ungodly ones, to be heard, his presence, as arbiter and guide, is soon reasserted and never forgotten.

Moreover, those subsequent invocations, whatever their implications in terms of the symbolic structure of the text, reinforce the narrator's standing. In Book 3 he is established in the tradition of the blind seer, whom the 'celestial Light' may privilege to see and tell 'things invisible to mortal sight' (3.54–5). The invocation to Book 7, besides establishing Milton as a figure in opposition to the current ascendency, once more asserts the special relationship he has with the Christian muse, who is equatable with the Holy Spirit (7.28–31; above, Chapter 1). The final invocation, in Book 9, explicitly differentiates *Paradise Lost* from pagan epic in terms of the true heroism of its material, dictated 'to me slumbering' in the muse's 'nightly visitation unimplored' (9.22–3). Milton, then, invests much in fashioning a version of himself as member of a tradition of pious recorders and as transcendent poet, privileged above all pagan epic writers.

Distinguishing epic from the novel (which, in his view, is a dialogic form in which voices other than that of the narrator may be fully heard), Bakhtin suggests that the essential difference is in the temporal relationship between the events and the narration of the events:

The epic, as the specific genre known to us today, has been from the beginning a poem about the past, and the authorial position immanent in the epic and constitutive of it (that is, the position of the one who utters the epic word) is the environment of a man speaking about the past that is to him inaccessible, the reverent point of view of a descendent. . . . The epic past . . . lacks any relativity, that is, any gradual, purely temporal progressions that might connect it with the present. It is walled off absolutely from all subsequent times, and above all from those times in which the singer and his listeners are located.[17]

The comments may well hold for Homeric epic, though Virgil's has a prophetic element which ties celebration of the founding of Rome to panegyric directed towards its current ruler. In Milton's case, however, Bakhtin's point is untenable. His Christian epic, in which all of human experience, even that which is yet to come, is linked, in no way walls off the past; rather, it asserts the transhistorical continuities of Christian belief. Bacon remarks that prophecy 'is but Divine History; which hath that prerogative over human [history], as the narration may be before the fact as well as after'.[18] That is, the status of events that are prophesied is conceptually indistinguishable from events that have occurred. Milton's narrative structure persistently shifts from the primary period of the story, the age of Adam and Eve, to earlier events, to events in Milton's age, to events that are in the future. History is all around us, even the history of events that are still to come, and if providence is to be our guide, so too is the narrative voice of Milton.

NOTES

1. F. K. Blessington, *'Paradise Lost' and the classical epic* (Boston, London and Henley: Routledge and Kegan Paul, 1979), p. ix.

2. Blessington, p. 104.

3. Joseph Addison and Richard Steele, *The Spectator*, edited by D. F. Bond (Oxford: Clarendon Press, 1965), Vol 3 p. 173; all references are to this edition and follow quotations in the text.

4. G. K. Hunter, *Paradise Lost* (London: Allen and Unwin, 1980), p. 15.

5. Hunter, especially pp. 14–30.

6.   Thomas N. Corns, *The Development of Milton's Style* (Oxford: Clarendon Press, 1982), p. 69.

7.   See Corns, *Milton's Language*, p. 97.

8.   Corns, *Milton's Language*, pp. 10–49.

9.   Harris F. Fletcher, (ed.), *John Milton's Complete Poetical Works Reproduced in Facsimile* (Urbana: University of Illinois Press, 1943–48), Vol 2 pp. 190–1; hereafter 'Facsimile edition'.

10. Facsimile edition, Vol 3 p. 68.

11. Campbell, p. 145.

12. Facsimile edition, Vol 3 p. 70.

13. These observations are based on the exhaustive statistical information gathered and analysed in Corns, *Development* and *Milton's Language*; readers seeking a fuller substantiation are directed to those works.

14. Christopher Ricks, *Milton's Grand Style* (1963; Oxford and New York: Oxford University Press, 1967), p. 73.

15. Fowler, pp. 22–5 and notes to 9.1–47; and Maren-Sofie Røstvig, *Configurations: A Topomorphical Approach to Renaissance Poetry* (forthcoming), Chapter 9.

16. Stanley E. Fish, *Surprised by Sin: the Reader in Paradise Lost* (London and New York: Macmillan and St Martin's Press, 1967), p. 22.

17. M. M. Bakhtin, *The Dialogic Imagination*, translated by Caryl Emerson and Michael Holquist, edited by Michael Holquist (Austin: University of Texas Press, 1981), pp. 13, 15; the issues are discussed more fully in Thomas N. Corns, '"That prerogative over human": *Paradise Lost* and the Telling of Divine History', in Roy T. Erikson, (ed.) (Berlin: Moulton de Gruyter, forthcoming, 1994).

18. Francis Bacon, *The Advancement of Learning*, edited by G. W. Kitchen (1861; London: Dent, 1965), p. 69.

Chapter 6

The Politics of *Paradise Lost*

In his own age Milton's reputation rested largely on his political writings. This chapter consolidates the political readings which pervade earlier chapters, and it completes my attempt to recontextualise *Paradise Lost* in the political milieu in which he lived and worked.

In 1629 Charles I resolved to rule without parliaments, and through the 1630s, the period of what is usually termed his 'personal rule', opposition to the practices and policies of the court had been extraparliamentary and, to some extent, covert.

The issues which exercised that opposition were numerous. Charles I's predilections in religion were for the ceremonial Anglicanism associated with William Laud, whom he made in turn bishop of London and archbishop of Canterbury. Like Milton (but unlike most puritans), Laud was an Arminian, rejecting Calvin's notion of the predestinate salvation or damnation of each individual in favour of a theory which held that salvation was open to all who would cooperate with the grace extended to them. In Milton's version of Arminianism, as we have seen (above, Chapter 3), that synergy is an intimate struggle between grace and the conscience, on one side, and the legacy of innate sinfulness on the other. In Laudian Arminianism, the ministry plays a major part, and the rituals and sacraments of the church work on the conscience, encouraging and confirming the regeneration of those who accede to the approach of grace.

Laud's version of Anglicanism brought him into sharp controversy within his church, and his views were enforced with the rigour of the law as well as with the sanctions available to him as archbishop. English puritanism had its origins in the Elizabethan period among those who felt that the Elizabethan church settlement retained too much of the ritual and the management structure of the Catholic church which Elizabeth had abolished. Laud, while deeply anti-Catholic, certainly gave a fresh militancy to that opposition by his insistence on church ritual, on the use of vestments distinguishing the clergy sharply from the laity, on the positioning of the altar within churches in such a way as to mark off and privilege the space appropriate to the clergy from the body of the churches where the laity could worship. Moreover, to enforce this cultural shift within the church Laud used and extended the hierarchical, top-down managerial structure of the church, which invested very considerable power in him as archbishop of Canterbury and in the bishops. This prelatical church-government as it was called, that is government of the church by bishops, became itself a target for puritan activists within the church; presbyterians, who were themselves Anglican communicants in the 1630s, argued for a system of church government much closer to that of Calvin's Genevan church, with a hierarchy of committees to determine the order of church services and to decide which doctrines were orthodox.

Within the church, the vigour of Laudian reform alienated not only those of a presbyterian leaning but also others who believed in prelatical church-government but retained a commitment to Calvinist theories of salvation and who disapproved, too, of some of the new emphasis on ritual. Outside the church, more militant puritans had already formed themselves into alternative 'separate' congregations, the precursors of the Independent congregation-alists and the sects of the mid-seventeenth century.

Quite a few puritan activists, alarmed by the prohibitions and threats they faced in England, withdrew into a sort of exile in continental Europe or the American colonies; those who remained faced sometimes very severe penalties if they persisted in puri-tanical criticism of the Church of England or the royal court that supported it. In 1634 William Prynne had his ears cut off for allegedly libelling the King and Queen; in 1637 John Bastwick and Henry Burton also had their ears cropped for disseminating puritan texts, and Prynne was facially branded and had the residual stumps of his ears cropped again. In 1638 the future Leveller leader, John Lilburne, was flogged from Fleet Prison to the pillory in Palace Yard for importing puritan books. All four were incarcerated in conditions which were life-threateningly harsh.

Those events probably played a crucial part in radicalising Milton. Before then, his poetry had been, politically, quite conservative. As a student, he had celebrated in Latin the anniversary of James I's escape from the Gunpowder Plot; as a young man, he had composed a masque, *Comus*, and an aristocratic entertainment, *Arcades*, for magnates close to the court. But his elegy, 'Lycidas', published in 1638, manifests a new public opposition to the Laudian ascendancy, albeit (with understandable caution) somewhat obliquely expressed.[1] When he reissued the poem after the collapse of Laud's domination, in his anthology of 1645, he made its ideological implications explicit in a headnote: it 'by occasion foretells the ruin of our corrupted clergy then in their height'.

Charles I managed to govern without recourse to a parliament by a twin policy of avoiding major expenditure on foreign adventures and raising revenue by fiscal stratagems of dubious legality. In 1639, however, the attempt to render a more Laudian aspect to religious observation in his Scottish kingdom involved him in protracted and unsuccessful military campaigns which brought with them the necessity of convening parliament to seek new revenue. The Long Parliament met in 1640, and thus those oppositional forces found the platform denied them in the years of personal rule.

Though moderate presbyterians and anti-Laudian episcopalians attempted to patch together a new compromise church settlement, Milton devoted himself to the cause of root-and-branch reform of the Church of England. The five pamphlets which he wrote in 1641–42 define eloquently the persona of his polemic; the authorial voice is violent, undeferential and implacable.

The aggression, though no doubt emanating from within Milton's personality, was purposeful. It sought to distance the supporters of prelacy from even the most moderate and appeasing elements of presbyterian puritanism and thus to render compromise impossible. It reflected, too, a powerful surge of millenarian optimism, a belief that Christ in judgement would settle with those who persecuted the godly and declare the thousand-year reign of the saints.

The English Civil War between the King and his supporters and the supporters of those in parliament who opposed him began in the summer of 1642. Though there is no evidence that Milton participated in the fighting (his brother appears in the *royalist* muster roll at Reading, however), he remained a political activist till the restoration of the monarchy in 1660.

We have considered some aspects of Milton's religious heterodoxy already. His active interrogation of received protestant doctrine found no abiding place among those moderate divines who dominated the spiritual landscape of London in the early 1640s. In 1643 he published a pamphlet calling for a reform of the divorce law in ways which would acknowledge kinds of breakdown of marriage other than adultery or non-consummation. The new puritan establishment roundly censured his book and attempted its suppression. In the controversy that followed, Milton, who found himself increasing aligned with more radical thinkers, produced what is now his most famous tract, *Areopagitica* (1644), calling for a considerable relaxation of the law of censorship as it related to the publication of works of religious controversy.

In the late 1640s, those radicals with whom Milton had become associated – we may best term them revolutionary Independents – displaced the ascendancy of the presbyterians and their allies, mainly through the rise of Cromwell and the officer corps of the New Model Army. Though the Civil War in effect ended   in parliamentarian victory with the battle of Naseby in 1645, fighting broke out again with royalist uprisings in 1647. Parliament, too, became increasingly mistrusted by the more radical officers of the parliamentary army, the New Model. A combination of events prompted Cromwell and the senior officers closest to him to march on London and to take the King, who had been handed over to parliament by the Scots to whom he had surrendered. Parliament was purged of less radical elements and the King was placed on trial. On 30 January 1649 he was beheaded.

Though Milton had been pushed to the periphery of English political life in the mid-1640s, in 1649 he entered into his most conspicuous phase. He produced a pamphlet justifying the trial of the King; he wrote in justification of Cromwell's invasion of Ireland; and he wrote the official republican reply to *Eikon Basilike*, Charles I's apologia, perhaps ghosted for him, but widely and influentially circulated in 1649–50. Milton entered the paid employment of the English republic, writing Latin defences of it to vindicate it before the governments and the intelligensia of Europe, as well as drafting diplomatic documents in Latin. In the late 1650s, though still receiving a salary, he functionally retired from public service, but in 1660 he produced, in the twilight of the republic, eloquent and immensely courageous pamphlets in opposition to the restoration of monarchy. At that restoration, few would have been surprised had he been among those executed.

THE LEGACY OF REVOLUTION

Milton's political career brought the experience both of ecstatic millenarian optimism and of the most abject of defeats. It was rooted in the grisly spectacular punishments of the 1630s; it ended in the grisly spectacular punishments of the 1660s. He always feared he would be assassinated by someone dissatisfied that he had escaped so lightly at the Restoration.[2] His political career is sometimes represented as an abberation from his vocation, his higher mission, to write the finest English epic. That view is wrong; the epic itself is permeated with a political consciousness shaped by the English revolution.

Thus, the concluding accounts of the godly baited by the mob, hounded and persecuted as the incarnate Son was persecuted, end the poem at a stage analogous to the way the English revolution had ended, and analogous to how Milton was living as he wrote the poem. The experience of defeat informs that haunted vision – not paranoid, because of course many of the old revolutionaries were persecuted – of the poet:

> fallen on evil days,
> On evil days though fallen, and evil tongues;
> In darkness, and with dangers compassed round,
> And solitude . . .

(7.25–8)

Milton's recurrent myth is of the solitary and persecuted, protected only by the spirit within, in the case of the poet in its aesthetic manifestation of the Christian muse. History repeats itself almost endlessly, and the story it tells is a story of, in Milton's phrase used in a late republican pamphlet, 'that which is not call'd amiss *the good Old Cause*' (*The Readie and Easie Way to Establish a Free Commonwealth, CPW*, 7, revised edition, 462). The cause becomes the bearing of witness to truth despite circumambient

and terrifying threats. In the decade of the English republic,
the state which Milton served allowed a freedom to speculative
intellects like Milton's in a way without precedent in England.
The old bullies and bugbears, the autocratic king, the hierarchical
and interdictive bishops, were pushed aside in what seemed by
mid-1660 a brief golden age unsustainable in the fallen world, and
suffering returned *sine die* as the price of godliness.

The major poems Milton published after *Paradise Lost* in the twin
volume of 1671, *Paradise Regained* and *Samson Agonistes*, celebrate
two other versions of the godly witness alone among powerful
enemies. Each carries a securer conviction of the ultimate defeat
of the reprobates. Thus, in *Paradise Regained* the incarnate Son
engages in protracted debate with Satan, unperturbed by Satan's
physical superiority. Satan attempts to terrify him with storms,
only to be dismissed with the human but potent directness of the
Son's response:

> Me worse than wet though find'st not; other harm
> Those terrors which thou speak'st of, did me none;
> I never feared they could.
>
> (4.486–8)

Set on the pinnacle, 'Tempt not the Lord thy God, he said and
stood./But Satan smitten with amazement fell' (4.561–2). By the
end of the poem, the Son, by reason of his courageous godliness,
has played over the conflicts of *Paradise Lost* and brought them
to a happier conclusion; as the angelic choir expresses it in their
heavenly anthem:

> now thou hast avenged
> Supplanted Adam, and, by vanquishing
> Temptation, hast regained lost Paradise,
> And frustrated the conquest fraudulent.
>
> (4.606–9)

Significantly, Milton locates the victory in the most human and
obscure episode of the life of the incarnate Son; he is a solitary
in a remote desert, and his success, which is wholly spiritual and
intellectual, is unwitnessed by other human beings. It is a victory
which forgoes the military and political means by which the Good
Old Cause had been promoted.

But the Son is the son of God; the hero of *Paradise Regained*'s
companion piece, Samson, manifests a more fragile humanity.

Once more, he is alone among his enemies. Blinded, imprisoned, humbled by servile toil, he is threatened with humiliation analogous to the spectacular punishment of the executed revolutionaries, exhibition at the feast to honour Dagon, '[t]he worst of indignities' (line 1341). Yet he resists as best he can, and he finds within him the necessary strength:

> Be of good courage, I begin to feel
> Some rousing motions in me which dispose
> To something extraordinary my thoughts.

(lines 1381–3)

To those familiar with Milton's characteristic representation of the Holy Spirit, these lines are easy enough to interpret. Samson, regaining something of his old guile, tells the officer charged with bringing him to the feast:

> I am content to go.
> Masters' commands come with a power resistless
> To such as owe them absolute subjection.

(lines 1403–5)

Of course, the reader knows, as the officer does not, that Samson (like all witnesses to the Good Old Cause) owes absolute subjection to only one master, the God who communicates to them through the Holy Spirit within. The modernised text, which inserts an apostrophe after 'Masters', rather spoils the ambiguity of the original, which reads 'Masters commands', which could as easily be the commands of one as of more masters.[3] Samson's triumph is more limited than the incarnate Son's, the bleaker satisfactions of revenge on the ungodly at the expense of his own life. He has left his enemies 'years of mourning' (line 1712). Those who question whether Milton endorses this bloody reverie may recall how he called for such reprisals in the years of the ascendancy of revolutionary Independency. The tone of the concluding exchanges in *Samson Agonistes* does not differ much from the tone of Milton's Sonnet 15, 'On the late Massacre in Piedmont', written at the height of Cromwell's power, which begins with the chilling prayer, 'Avenge, O Lord thy slaughtered saints, whose bones/Lie scattered on the Alpine mountains cold'. Forgiveness never figures significantly as a motif in Milton's creative or polemic repertoire.

Yet the poems published in 1671 belong to a different moment in the history of Restoration non-conformity (as puritanism came to be termed). By then, the old radicals had endured and had survived a decade of persecution. With that came the recognition that they could and would survive; ideological extinction had been avoided. Those who had fought in that intellectual rearguard, though they had taken many casualties in the prisons of Restoration England as well as in more spectacular ways, and though they had suffered many desertions to the new order, had by the turn of the decade a new sense of the returning powers of the godly. Indeed, though Charles II had called in 1669 for renewed vigour in prosecuting the secret meetings of non-conformists, and the Cavalier Parliament in its winter session of 1670–71 persisted in its hard line, a change in policy was imminent; in 1672 Charles issued the Declaration of Indulgence, suspending all penal laws against dissenters.[4] Other dissenters manifested in the early 1670s a reanimated sense of political and spiritual potential; for example, Bunyan's writings from that time onward show a new polemical and evangelical edge.[5]

Though *Paradise Lost* was reissued in 1674, Milton's revisions were structural rather than ideological, and it remains a dissenter document of the 1660s. It memorialises not victory but defeat. In other realms, in the triumph over the fallen angels in the war in heaven and in their humiliating metamorphosis in hell, the godly, pre-eminently the pre-incarnate Son, may crush Satan and his legions; but in the earthly realm humankind loses a crucial struggle. The immediate consequence is exile; in prospect lies murder and persecution. By the end of the book Adam and Eve are as godly as the puritan saints, as godly as Milton presumably perceived himself to be, and they feel the Holy Spirit within them. But they are impotent against the forces which, as Michael reveals, will all but overwhelm them. The strategies available to them, including the newly valorised defensive formation of the nuclear family, are strategies for surviving, not for winning. Even the incarnation little changes godly humankind's objective conditions. In Milton's early Christmas poem, 'On the Morning of Christ's Nativity', an epoch ends and another begins so triumphantly that nature momentarily thinks the millennium has arrived. In *Paradise Lost*, the incarnation scarcely interrupts the experience of the postlapsarian nightmare, and it ushers in an epoch of intensified persecution (12.485; see above, Chapter 3).

The larger perspectives of the poem, with its intense short-term pessimism and its remotely long-term optimism, wholly match the temper of English non-conformity in the 1660s; by 1671 and the publication of *Samson Agonistes* and *Paradise Regained* other perspectives become once more tenable.

THE POLITICAL ANIMAL

Not only does Milton write as one profoundly shaped by the experience of mid-century radical politics, but he writes as one familiar with the ways of politicians and accomplished in the idiom of political polemic. As Latin Secretary, Milton stood very close to the centre of power in the English republic. He attended as a civil servant some of the meetings of the Council of State and of its subcommittees and working parties, and he knew numerous politicians with varying degrees of intimacy. John Bradshaw, for example, was his solicitor and probably a personal friend. Bradshaw had presided over the court which condemned Charles I to death, and his body was exhumed and gibbeted, along with Cromwell's, after the restoration. He would seem to have known Sir Henry Vane and addressed to him a sonnet. Vane, of aristocratic family, functioned as a maverick radical in the 1650s, and was beheaded in 1662. Milton's poem first appeared in an account of Vane's life and death published to coincide with the execution.

Some politicians Milton both knew and disliked. In 1651–52 a German diplomat negotiating a treaty on behalf of the state of Oldenburg made a journal of his meetings with Milton, who acted in the matter for the English republic. The account, which has been properly recovered only recently, records a certain asperity in Milton's less guarded comments about his political masters. Apologising for an error made by the Council, he remarked on:

> the inexperience and willfulness of those who enjoyed the plurality of votes; those men mechanics, soldiers, homegrown, strong and bold enough, in public political affairs mostly inexperienced . . . among the forty persons who were in the Council, not more than three or four had ever been out of England.[6]

Christopher Hill, whose account of the political implications of *Paradise Lost* remains profoundly persuasive,[7] remarks on the relationship between the political institutions depicted in the poem and those extant in mid-century England. Certainly, the world of the fallen angels has certain parallels with the English republic. Thus, the larger body, in the early 1650s the Rump Parliament, supposedly supported (but in effect was often controlled by) a smaller Council of State, containing the more powerful army officers and leading civilian politicians, and dominated by Cromwell; so the mass of angels congregate (in miniature) in Pandaemonium, but:

> far within
> And in their own dimensions like themselves
> The great seraphic lords and cherubim
> In close recess and secret conclave sat . . .
>
> (1.792–5)

And above them all, in bad eminence, Satan. I am not suggesting that Books 1 and 2 constitute a jaundiced *roman à clef* in which the leaders and the institutions of the English republic are equated with the Satanic forces; rather, Milton in depicting the political economy of hell does so in terms of a political economy with which he was familiar, indeed in which he had been a (peripheral) participant.

Moreover, Milton, extrapolating Satanic politics from the politics he knew, depicts the debate in hell in terms of gambits and stratagems of a human kind. Thus the proposal which concludes the debate in hell is advanced not by Satan but by Beelzebub, whose gravity and status are respected (2.300–9), and who seems to have no personal interest at stake. However, he formulates a policy, the corruption of the newly formed world, in terms which give Satan an advantage over the other leading rebels, in that he knows what is coming and has thought through his response. At the end of Beelzebub's speech, his peers are convinced: 'joy/Sparkled in all their eyes; with full assent/They vote' (2.387–9). But Milton cautions those readers who have shared those rebels' delusions, observing that Satan has prepared Beelzebub for this role: 'Thus Beelzebub/Pleaded his devilish counsel, first devised/By Satan, and in part proposed' (2.377–9). Once Satan has volunteered for the mission of first searching 'this new world' (2.403), he hastens to conclude the meeting:

> Thus saying rose
> The monarch, and prevented all reply,
> Prudent, lest from his resolution raised

> Others among the chief might offer now
> (Certain to be refused) what erst they feared;
> And so refused might in opinion stand
> His rivals, winning cheap the high repute
> Which he through hazard huge must earn.
>
> (2.466–73)

Note that Satan's conduct is pre-emptive, a guileful stratagem designed to forestall the slightly less guileful stratagem he is anticipating.

We need not assume that Milton is modelling the debate on any particular incidents of the Council of State; for Satan, we need not read Cromwell, for Beelzebub, we need not read one or other of his allies. Indeed, anyone with some familiarity with student or faculty politics, local government, committee work in neighbourhood organisations or pressure groups may well feel at home with the political discourse of Milton's hell. Again, while we know that Milton's experience of such manoeuvres was first-hand, it could as easily have been derived from Sir Francis Bacon's influential and much reprinted writing on matters of state. For example, his essay 'Of Cunning' contains numerous ruses (though not the specific ones used in Book 2):

> [S]urprise may be made by moving things when the party is in haste, and cannot stay to consider advisedly of this is moved.
>
> If a man would cross a business that he doubts some other would handsomely and effectually move, let him pretend to wish it well, and move it himself in such sort as may foil it.
>
> The breaking off in the midst of that one was about to say, as if he took himself up, breeds a greater appetite in him with whom you confer to know more.
>
> And because it works better when anything seemeth to be gotten from you by question, than if you offer it of yourself, you may lay a bait for a question, by shewing another visage and countenance than you are wont; to the end to give occasion for the party to ask what the matter is of the change? . . .
>
> I knew one that, when he wrote a letter, he would put that which was most material in the postscript, as if it had been a by-matter.

And so through other ruses. Bacon concludes, in implausibly pious vein, 'these small wares and petty points of cunning are infinite; and it were a good deed to make a list of them; for that nothing doth more hurt in a state than that cunning men pass for wise'.[8]

But in *Paradise Lost* such small wares are not exclusively the property of the fallen. The godly – even the Godhead – may use guile. Indeed, as we have seen, the politic control of information is central to orchestration of the tests faced by Satan and by Adam and Eve. Even the abrasive and disruptive suddenness with which the Father discloses and anoints the Son reflects a kind of double guile. Of course, on the human scale and in the earthly realm it would be unwise to proceed in a manner likely to cause the maximum resentment; but to test the angels' obedience, the Father needs to cause exactly that outrage among those who fall. God is no courtier.

Nor does he always tell all that is pertinent. Again, we should recall that Satan and the fallen angels operate from erroneous premises because of the Godhead's guileful retention of information. Thus, their escape from the fiery lake in Book 1, like Satan's solitary egress from hell in Book 2, is permissive, though they do not perceive it in those terms. Similarly, they misinterpret why God postponed their defeat in the war in heaven, thus taking the comfort they needed to motivate themselves in their oppositional course of action, which in turn serves God's purpose. For Milton, the practice of politics, perhaps like that of rhetoric, was ethically neutral, and the godly needed to master it, for good ends, to match the accomplishment of the forces of evil.

REPUBLICAN AND ANTI-CLERICAL VALUES

We have seen how Milton defines the fall of Satan essentially as a political crime, a kind of tyranny in that it is a revolt against the Father and the Son who are truly superior beings (see chapter 2). Satan's ungodly republicanism is to be differentiated from the republicanism of the English saints, who acknowledged that God alone is rightly king. Persistently, however, Satan and his political agenda are associated not with republicanism but with kingship. In passage after passage Satan in particular is termed a king, and he is linked with the excesses of historical kingship.[9]

The style of kingship associated with Satan is exotic, profligate, unreasonable and barbaric. Thus, at the onset of the 'great consult' (1.798), he is enthroned thus:

> High on a throne of a royal state, which far
> Outshone the wealth of Ormus and of Ind,

> Or where the gorgeous East with richest hand
> Showers on her kings barbaric pearl and gold,
> Satan exalted sat, by merit raised
> To that bad eminence . . .

(2.1–6)

As Fowler notes, Satan has already been portrayed as an eastern tyrant, 'their great sultan' (1.348; Fowler 2.1–4n.). Quite so; but the outlandishness the description evokes had its recent English analogues. On St George's Day, 1661:

> the government staged Charles [II]'s English coronation. 'Staged' is the appropriate verb, as historical precedent was studied and developed to produce royal pageantry of breath-taking spendour. The robes of one peer were said to have cost £30,000, Hyde [Charles's chief minister at this time] 'shone like a diamond', and an onlooker wondered how [so] many ostrich feathers could have been found in England.[10]

You can see, too, the Satanic pomp depicted in contemporary illustrations of the event.[11] In *The Readie and Easie Way* Milton had warned that 'a king must be ador'd like a Demigod, with a dissolute and haughtie court about him, of vast expence and luxurie' (*CPW*, 7, revised edition, 425). In the England of the 1660s the oriental exoticism of Satan's throne may have seemed to have found a domestic equivalent.

John Toland, an early biographer of Milton, notes that the Licenser, who was required to vet the book under the press controls which obtained after the restoration, 'among other frivolous Exceptions, would needs suppress the whole Poem for imaginary Treason in the following lines',[12]

> as when the sun new risen
> Looks through the horizontal misty air
> Shorn of his beams, or from behind the moon
> In dim eclipse disastrous twilight sheds
> On half the nations, and with fear of change
> Perplexes monarchs.

(1.594–9)

Sadly, we do not know which other passages caught the censor's eye. Here, however, Toland's condescending dismissal seems unfounded (or is perhaps disingenuous). Milton persistently in *Paradise Lost* operates on the edge of what was permissible, and, though creative writing generally in the mid-century received slighter attention from the authorities than polemic or news (after all many royalist poets published with impunity in the 1640s and 1650, while newsbooks were rigorously suppressed), Milton as a notorious old revolutionary could reasonably have expected his poem to receive more careful attention than it would had another written it. The dubious simile once more links Satan – it is describing his obscured glory – with kingship. Moreover, it suggests that kingship, far from being eternal and natural, is an unstable institution, and that, throughout the world, the current monarchs may not reign for ever. Flux and change were conditions the restored Stuarts tried hard to distance from the public perception of their reign.

Such numerous small-scale insinuations of republican values pervade the epic. So, too, do the values of anti-clericalism. Milton's earliest prose polemic had been in attack on the bishops who dominated the Church of England and in defence and support of a group of five presbyterian divines, who, under the acronym taken from their initials, SMECTYMNUUS, had engaged a leading prelatical apologist in debate. Once Milton's more heterodox writing attracted the hostility of presbyterians and their allies in the mid-1640s, his antiprelaticism extended into a much broader rejection of a paid, professional clergy. Presbyter and Laudian priest seemed but two manifestations of the same repressive corruption. As he put it in 'On the New Forcers of Conscience under the Long Parliament', a short poem of the mid-1640s, 'New *Presbyter* is but old *Priest* writ large' (line 20), quibbling on the fact that 'priest' is etymologically a contracted form of 'presbyter', a Latin word for 'elder'. The term 'priest' was widely used in seventeenth-century English for the clergy of the Church of England, especially in their role as officiants at the Eucharists and other sacerdotal offices; it occurs frequently in the Book of Common Prayer; though it was also used of those performing sacerdotal roles in non-Christian religions.[13]

Milton's use of the word is not always opprobrious. Thus, just as the Son is a true king, so he is a true priest, and he terms himself 'thy priest' as he presents the prayers of the penitent Adam and Eve to the Father (11.25). More generally, Milton playfully emphasises the corrupt transhistorical role of the beneficed priesthood, jumbling together pagan and Jewish and Christian in a compound image of venality and unreliability. Though the message is cryptically encoded, the anti-clerical values are clear enough. Thus, the fallen

angels who later manifest themselves on earth as false gods are ably
seconded by the professional clergy:

> A crew who under names of old renown,
> Osiris, Isis, Orus and their train
> With monstrous shapes and sorceries abused
> Fanatic Egypt and her priests, to seek
> Their wandering gods disguised in brutish forms.
>
> (1.477–81)

Again, Belial establishes a special relationship with the professional
clergy:

> Belial came last, than whom a spirit more lewd
> Fell not from heaven, or more gross to love
> Vice for itself: to him no temple stood
> Or altar smoked; yet who more oft than he
> In temples and at altars, when the priest
> Turns atheist, as did Ely's sons, who filled
> With lust and violence the house of God.
> In courts and palaces he also reigns
> And in luxurious cities . . .
>
> (1.490–8)

Note the tense of the verbs, '[t]urns' and 'reigns'. The specific
example he cites, that of the sons of Eli, relates to an episode
from Old Testament history, in which corrupt priests stole what
was intended as a sacrifice and 'lay with the women that assembled
at the door of the tabernacle of the congregation' (1 Sam. 2:12–4:11).
The present tense indicates that the phenomenon which Eli's sons
illustrate is continuous, presumably in all societies which invest
powers in a carnal clergy, just as the spirit of Belial continues
to infect (all?) courts and palaces, with its blow aimed at the
sexual mores of the court of Charles II. Since the sons of Eli
were later killed during an episode of national disgrace, there may
be a subdued element of prophecy or wishful thinking. As in
his comments differentiating married chastity from court amours
(4.765–70; discussed above, Chapter 3), Milton's text still speaks to
the cognoscenti the language of the Good Old Cause, though its
tones are somewhat hushed.

   In a tract of 1659 Milton had termed all professional clergy –
he is plainly thinking of puritan divines – sons of Eli in their
rapaciousness (*The Likeliest Means to Remove Hirelings out of the*

Church, CPW, 7, rev. ed., 296), and he may well be aiming at the puritan clergy, especially those of presbyterian persuasion, in his last anti-clerical gesture in *Paradise Lost*, his account of the role of the priesthood in the catastrophe of the Jewish civilisation after its return from Babylon:

> grown
> In wealth and multitude, factious they grow;
> But first among the priests dissension springs,
> Men who attend the altar, and should most
> Endeavour peace: their strife pollution brings
> Upon the Temple it self: at last they seize
> The sceptre . . .
>
> (12.351–7)

Milton may be intending that his readers recall the disruptiveness of Laud in the years leading to the outbreak of war; however, the idiom seems closest to that heard repeatedly in Milton's republican pamphlets of 1649 and especially in *The Tenure of Kings and Magistrates*, where he charges the presbyterian clergy with initiating conflicts with the king that they later disavowed and with continuing to ferment political discord by opposing the republican state settlement (see *CPW*, 3.232–33, 240, for example).

But Milton's anti-clericalism is most eloquently manifested not in what he says but in his silences. Most significantly, and in a way which sharply differentiates radical Arminianism from Laudian Arminianism, ritual and the roles of the mediators are excluded from Adam and Eve's devotions and from their spiritual regeneration. A major issue of contention between a broad spectrum of puritan opinion and the Laudian ascendancy had been the twin insistence that extemporary prayer be inhibited and that the forms of the Book of Common Prayer be uniformly adopted. Milton often articulated the puritan belief that prayer without an interior prompting was fruitless. As he puts it in *Eikonoklastes*,

> Much less can it be lawfull that an Englisht Mass-Book [i.e., the Book of Common Prayer] . . . *deprive* us the exercise of that Heav'nly gift, which God by special promise powrs out daily upon his Church, that is to say, the spirit of Prayer. Wherof . . . we have a remedy of Gods finding out, which is not Liturgie, but his own free spirit. Though we know not what to pray as we ought, yet he with sighs unutterable by any words, much less by a stinted Liturgie, dwelling in us makes

intercession for us, according to the mind and will of God, both in privat, and in the performance of all Ecclesiastical duties.

(*CPW*, 3.507)

Paradise Lost has its prayers and its rituals, but they are characterised by their interiority, by their inner spiritual prompting.

Thus, at evening Adam and Eve pray spontaneously but in unison – and they pray standing up, without the kneeling rituals of the Book of Common Prayer (4.720–35): 'This said unanimous, and other rites/Observing none, but adoration pure/Which God likes best' (4.736–8). There is a special anti-clerical frisson in Milton's next use of the word 'rites', six lines later, in allusion to sexual intercourse.

We have seen already the role of the Son as the true priest, the sole mediator between the Father and humankind. If Adam and Eve may experience regeneration without the rituals and the sacraments of the Church, then (the silence implies) so too may all fallen people who respond to the spirit within.

Paradise Lost, politically, remains a deeply pessimistic text; but it is also still a deeply subversive one. The value it places on interiority, on obeying and trusting the promptings of the spirit, ultimately denies all loyalties to any institution of the state. No legitimate hierarchy stands between any believer and his or her God. The clergy are at best redundant; at worst, venal, repressive, self-seeking, and available to aid the tyrant's whim. Kings and their courts rise and fall, despite their ancient claims and dynasties; while they rule, they persecute and suppress the godly, over whose consciences they can have no sustainable claim. Even the people, in *Paradise Lost*, the mass of the ordinary godly citizen's reprobate peers, may not be trusted. They throng around the isolated saint, much as the rebel angels mob Abdiel, the godly remnant of their band. But the individual who heeds the inner spirit may endure; the Good Old Cause can be defeated, but it cannot be destroyed. As Bunyan put it, 'Who would true Valour see/Let him come hither'.[14] Or in Wordsworth's phrase, 'Milton! Thou should'st be living in this hour.'[15]

NOTES

1.   John Leonard, '"Trembling ears": the historical moment of *Lycidas*', *Journal of Medieval and Renaissance Studies*, 21 (1991), pp. 59–81.

2. Parker, 1.562, p. 577.

3. Facsimile edition, 4.273.

4. Ronald Hutton, *Charles II, King of England, Scotland, and Ireland* (1989; Oxford: Oxford University Press, 1991), pp. 267, 275, 284–5.

5. Thomas N. Corns, 'Bunyan's *Grace Abounding* and the Dynamics of Restoration Nonconformity', in Neil Rhodes, (ed.) *History, Language, the Politics of English Renaissance Prose* (Binghamton: MRTS, forthcoming).

6. Leo Miller, *John Milton and the Oldenburg Safeguard* (New York: Loewenthal Press, 1985), p. 172.

7. Christopher Hill, *Milton and the English Revolution* (London: Faber, 1977), especially Chapter 29.

8. Francis Bacon, *Essays* (1906; London and New York: J. M. Dent and E. P. Dutton, 1966), pp. 68–9, 71.

9. For a full and fine account of the issues, see Stevie Davies, *Images of Kingship in 'Paradise Lost': Milton's Politics and Christian Liberty* (Columbia, Missouri: University of Missouri Press, 1983).

10. Hutton, pp. 164–5.

11. For example, Dirk Stoop, *The Coronation of Charles II* (private collection), reproduced in Blair Worden, (ed.), *Stuart England* (Oxford: Phaidon, 1986), pp. 148–9.

12. Darbishire, p. 189.

13. *OED*, s. v. 'priest 8, n.; *EOED2*, searched on quotation, 1600–1700.

14. Bunyan, p. 385.

15. William Wordsworth, 'London, 1802', line 1, in *Poetical Works*, edited by Thomas Hutchinson and revised by Ernest de Selincourt (1936; Oxford: Oxford University Press, 1967), p. 244.

Further Reading

11. Empson, William, *Milton's God*, second edition (London: Chatto and Windus, 1961).
The most significant monograph in the history of Milton criticism and a challenging attack both on the Christian tradition in Milton studies and on Christianity itself. It argues that Milton's epic, far from justifying the ways of God to man, anatomises the injustices inherent in Christian belief. See items 3 and 8.

12. Fish, Stanley Eugene, *Surprised by Sin: the Reader in Paradise Lost* (London and New York: Macmillan and St Mart... Press, 1967).
This book placed the reader's interpretative strategies o... agenda in Milton studies. The issues remain pertinent a... arguments and the local readings retain their cogency.

13. Hill, Christopher, *Milton and the English Revolution* (... Faber, 1977).
The only recent study of Milton by a first-rank h... contextualises Milton's writing in the English radic... establishing connections with the extremer sect... mid-century. Includes a useful reading of the ... nificance of the later poetry.

14. Hunter, G. K., *'Paradise Lost'* (London: Alle... 1980).
An urbane and informed introduction to the ...

15. Keeble, N. H., *The Literary Culture of Non... Seventeenth-Century England* (Leicester: Le... Press, 1987).
The best account of how Milton and o... negotiated the ideological crises posed ... Fixes well the cultural and religious mil...

16. Leonard, John, *Naming in Paradise: M... Adam and Eve* (Oxford: Clarendon Pr... A fine close reading of the poem, e... comments on Adam and Eve and th...

17. Lewis, C. S., *A Preface to Para...* (London and New York: Oxford...

a
to
of re
ductio

3. Fowler,
English Po
frequently re
Modernised s,
the best edition
Milton, edited by
Annotated English
Green, and Co., 196
which has also been pu
indeed. Fowler's annotat
arguments of earlier critics
11, below) with finesse and

A spirited and influential Christian reading, delivered with some panache. Quite useful on Milton's place in the epic tradition.

18. Lieb, Michael, *Poetics of the Holy: A Reading of* Paradise Lost (Chapel Hill: University of North Carolina Press, 1981). A sensitive account of the religious power of the poem.

19. Loewenstein, David, *Milton and the Drama of History: Historical Vision, Iconoclasm, and the Literary Imagination* (Cambridge and New York: Cambridge University Press, 1990). An intelligent application of Hayden White's theories to Milton studies; particularly useful for appreciating the closing books of *Paradise Lost*.

20. McColley, Diane K., *Milton's Eve* (Urbana: University of Illinois Press, 1983). Probably the best book on Eve and the gender politics of the poem.

21. Milner, Andrew, *John Milton and the English Revolution* >F7 (London and Basingstoke: Macmillan, 1981). Especially perceptive on the ideology of Revolutionary Independency; useful for understanding the political argument of the poem.

22. Parker, William Riley, *Milton: A Biography*, second edition, revised by Gordon Campbell (1968; Oxford: Clarendon, 1994). Still the best current biography of Milton, now revised to incorporate more recent scholarship, especially relating to Milton's work as Latin Secretary.

23. Revard, Stella, *The War in Heaven:* Paradise Lost *and the Tradition of Satan's Rebellion* (Ithaca and London: Cornell University Press, 1980). A valuable account of the middle books of the poem.

24. Schwartz, Regina, *Remembering and Repeating: Biblical Creation in* Paradise Lost (Cambridge and New York: Cambridge University Press, 1988). Wider in its range than the title suggests; particularly stimulating in its discussion of Chaos and the Creation.

25. Turner, James Grantham, *One Flesh: Paradisal Marriage and Sexual Relations in the Age of Milton* (Oxford and New York: Clarendon, 1987).

A full account of Milton's depiction of the relationship of Adam and Eve in the context of contemporary theories about prelapsarian sexuality.

Index of Passages Discussed

The reader may use this index to find discussions of particular passages of *Paradise Lost*. The index is divided into the original Book Numbers with the passages for discussion listed under these Book Numbers. The figures in the adjacent column refer to page numbers in this volume.

Paradise Lost

Thus I departed from them [in the courtroom]; and I can truly say, I bless the Lord *Jesus Christ* for it, that my heart was sweetly refreshed in the time of my examination, and also afterwards, at my returning to the prison: So that I found *Christ's* words more than bare trifles, where he saith, he *will give a mouth and wisdom, even such as all the adversaries shall not resist, or gainsay.* And that his peace no man can take from us.[27]

Bunyan's position, of survival through the interiorisation of religious experience and the development of inner strength, exemplifies a response wholly characteristic of Restoration non–conformity.[28] It accords well with the strategies of ideological resistance which Milton explores in the lives of the godly in the concluding books of epic (see chapters 3 and 6).

The Holy Spirit, though rarely manifest as a discrete presence or agent, figures very significantly in the vision of Godhead *Paradise Lost* develops. I have noted how the millenarian instinct, so strongly felt in early Milton, was displaced in the 1660s by a sense of the almost infinite postponement of the millennium. Now and for as long as Milton can foresee the godly remnant must endure in a world made intensely hostile to them. But they survive because they feel the Spirit within. In a sense, this, the fallen world, is the place and the age of that Spirit; with the rest of the Godhead now so distanced, with heaven a long way off and victory projected into remote futurity, it is the component of the Trinity available to wayfaring Christians; its pervasive force within them maintains them in their utmost extremity.

NOTES

1.   Unless stated, all references to *Paradise Lost* are to John Milton, *Paradise Lost*, edited by Alastair Fowler, Longman Annotated English Poets (London and New York: Longman, 1971) (hereafter Fowler).

2.   Geoffrey Chaucer, *The House of Fame*, lines 887–1090, in *The Works of Geoffrey Chaucer*, edited by F. N. Robinson, second edition (1957; London: Oxford University Press, 1968).

3.   Abraham Cowley, 'The Extasie', stanza 11, *The English Writing of Abraham Cowley*, edited by A. R. Waller (Cambridge: Cambridge University Press, 1905), p. 206.

     The Trial of Charles I (1964; London: The Reprint ... Pepys, *The Diary of Samuel Pepys*, edited ... Bell, 1970), I.265.

5.   B. S. Capp, *T*
     Millenarianism (

6.   On the ideolog
     see Chapter 6, b

7.   Lines 139–40; al
     edition in *The*
     Fowler, Longmar

8.   All references to
     edited by Don M.
     (hereafter *CPW* and

9.   Especially Romans
     Version of the Bible

10. *OED* 4 a and 2; Fow

11. William Empson, *Mil*
     1965), p. 126.

12. *CPW* 3.52; Blair Word
     Past and Present 109 (19

13. Achsah Guibbory, *The*
     Ideas of Pattern in History
     1986), p. 1; the range o
     Patrides, *Premises and Mc*
     Princeton University Pres

14. R. Buick Knox, *James U*
     Wales Press, 1967), p. 76.

15. Thomas N. Corns, *Unclois*
     (Oxford: Clarendon Press,

16. For an account of the discov
     and William B. Hunter, 'Th
     from the Bishop of Salisbu
     (1993), pp. 191–207.

17. See, especially, W. B. Hunter, C. A. Patrides, and J. H. Adamson, *Bright*
     Essence (Salt Lake City: University of Utah Press, 1971); Gordon Campbell,
     'The Son of God in *De Doctrina Christiana* and *Paradise Lost*,' *Modern Language*
     Review, 75 (1980), pp. 507–14; and '*De Doctrina Christiana*: Its Structura
     Principles and Unfinished State', *Milton Studies*, 9 (1976), pp. 24?

18. William B. Hunter, op. cit., and 'The P
     Studies in English Literature 15